The recess; or, a tale of other times. By the author of The chapter of accidents. The third edition, corrected. Volume 3 of 3

Sophia Lee

The recess; or, a tale of other times. By the author of The chapter of accidents. The third edition, corrected. Volume 3 of 3
Lee, Sophia
ESTCID: T069142
Reproduction from British Library
Dedication signed: Sophia Lee.
London : printed for T. Cadell, 1787.
3v. ; 8°

Gale ECCO Print Editions

Relive history with *Eighteenth Century Collections Online*, now available in print for the independent historian and collector. This series includes the most significant English-language and foreign-language works printed in Great Britain during the eighteenth century, and is organized in seven different subject areas including literature and language; medicine, science, and technology; and religion and philosophy. The collection also includes thousands of important works from the Americas.

The eighteenth century has been called "The Age of Enlightenment." It was a period of rapid advance in print culture and publishing, in world exploration, and in the rapid growth of science and technology – all of which had a profound impact on the political and cultural landscape. At the end of the century the American Revolution, French Revolution and Industrial Revolution, perhaps three of the most significant events in modern history, set in motion developments that eventually dominated world political, economic, and social life.

In a groundbreaking effort, Gale initiated a revolution of its own: digitization of epic proportions to preserve these invaluable works in the largest online archive of its kind. Contributions from major world libraries constitute over 175,000 original printed works. Scanned images of the actual pages, rather than transcriptions, recreate the works ***as they first appeared.***

Now for the first time, these high-quality digital scans of original works are available via print-on-demand, making them readily accessible to libraries, students, independent scholars, and readers of all ages.

For our initial release we have created seven robust collections to form one the world's most comprehensive catalogs of 18th century works.

Initial Gale ECCO Print Editions collections include:

History and Geography
Rich in titles on English life and social history, this collection spans the world as it was known to eighteenth-century historians and explorers. Titles include a wealth of travel accounts and diaries, histories of nations from throughout the world, and maps and charts of a world that was still being discovered. Students of the War of American Independence will find fascinating accounts from the British side of conflict.

Social Science

Delve into what it was like to live during the eighteenth century by reading the first-hand accounts of everyday people, including city dwellers and farmers, businessmen and bankers, artisans and merchants, artists and their patrons, politicians and their constituents. Original texts make the American, French, and Industrial revolutions vividly contemporary.

Medicine, Science and Technology

Medical theory and practice of the 1700s developed rapidly, as is evidenced by the extensive collection, which includes descriptions of diseases, their conditions, and treatments. Books on science and technology, agriculture, military technology, natural philosophy, even cookbooks, are all contained here.

Literature and Language

Western literary study flows out of eighteenth-century works by Alexander Pope, Daniel Defoe, Henry Fielding, Frances Burney, Denis Diderot, Johann Gottfried Herder, Johann Wolfgang von Goethe, and others. Experience the birth of the modern novel, or compare the development of language using dictionaries and grammar discourses.

Religion and Philosophy

The Age of Enlightenment profoundly enriched religious and philosophical understanding and continues to influence present-day thinking. Works collected here include masterpieces by David Hume, Immanuel Kant, and Jean-Jacques Rousseau, as well as religious sermons and moral debates on the issues of the day, such as the slave trade. The Age of Reason saw conflict between Protestantism and Catholicism transformed into one between faith and logic -- a debate that continues in the twenty-first century.

Law and Reference

This collection reveals the history of English common law and Empire law in a vastly changing world of British expansion. Dominating the legal field is the *Commentaries of the Law of England* by Sir William Blackstone, which first appeared in 1765. Reference works such as almanacs and catalogues continue to educate us by revealing the day-to-day workings of society.

Fine Arts

The eighteenth-century fascination with Greek and Roman antiquity followed the systematic excavation of the ruins at Pompeii and Herculaneum in southern Italy; and after 1750 a neoclassical style dominated all artistic fields. The titles here trace developments in mostly English-language works on painting, sculpture, architecture, music, theater, and other disciplines. Instructional works on musical instruments, catalogs of art objects, comic operas, and more are also included.

THE

RECESS;

OR, A

TALE OF OTHER TIMES.

THE

RECESS;

OR, A

TALE OF OTHER TIMES.

BY THE AUTHOR

OF THE

CHAPTER OF ACCIDENTS.

THE THIRD EDITION, CORRECTED.

"Are not these Woods
"More free from peril than the envious Court?
"Here feel we but the penalty of Adam,
"The seasons' difference."

VOL. III.

LONDON:
Printed for T. CADELL, in the Strand.
M.DCC.LXXXVII.

THE

RECESS, &c.

WHEN the sick languor of the faintings gave place to reflection, I found myself in my own bed; whither I understood I had been conveyed by the orders of Lord Arlington, as soon as my wound was staunched: his proved so slight that it left him no pretence for apprehension. Eagerly I enquired for Lady Pembroke, when to my inexpressible rage and astonishment I was informed, that she had been turned from my door; whither friendship had led her to venture a repulſe. The immaculate character of that admirable woman I thought even Lord Arlington would have reſpected, but without deigning to inform himſelf of the real circumſtances of the unforeſeen interview he had ſo dreadfully interrupted, he by this rude implication treated two of the moſt eſtimable and diſtinguiſhed perſons in the kingdom as abettors, if not contrivers of his diſhonour.—The little blood left in my veins turned to gall at the idea. I watched an opportunity to tear away the bandages; and diſdainfully reſigning myſelf to a premature fate, endeavoured to forget the generous hearts this raſh action would pierce.—The awful God, whoſe juſtice I thus queſtioned, ſtill extended to me his mercy—my dangerous ſituation was diſcovered in time by my careful attendants, who, infinitely more attached to me than to their Lord, uſed every means to prolong the life he, perhaps, wiſhed at its period.

In the cruel ſtate of mind which dictated this deſperate reſolution, it proved a me-a melancholy advantage; as the injury now fell on my constitution only, and my intellects escaped. It was many months ere I had strength to cross a room, or spirits to venture a question—during this memorable interval I called together every enfeebled power, and placing my conscience as umpire between myself and Lord Arlington, fixed and ascertained the rights of either. Convicted even by my own heart of imprudence, I wondered not that he construed error into guilt, and while thus cool offered him every vindication of my innocence he could reasonably desire: but Lord Arlington was the slave of passion and caprice, and not having firmness of soul to form, or fix, a judgment, he followed through years with invincible obstinacy the impression of the first moment.—From this period he ever treated me as an artful woman, whose licentious conduct had obliged him to risque his life in vain defence of that honor already sullied; and lost in my person; nor did he affect to assert his legal rights from any other reason than to separate me from Essex. This conduct, and the misrepresentations of Lady Essex, blazed the fatal incident throughout the Court, and fixed a stain on my character time could never erase—happily that stain reached not my person or my heart, and an injustice so aggravating on the part of Lord Arlington entitled me to forgive the little error in myself which occasioned it.

In this conjuncture I once more turned my tearful eyes every way around in search of a protector to interfere between me and a fate alike unmerited and severe.—Alas! there was not a human being virtue allowed me to call to my aid; and I exercised the faculties heaven had so unexpectedly blessed me with, by resolving to suffer with patience.

Elizabeth Vernon (our old companion), the fair and gentle cousin of Lord Essex, resolved if possible to see me—she ad-

dressed

dreſſed Lord Arlington, and demanded that privilege; the favour ſhe held with the Queen prevented his denying a requeſt he granted with the utmoſt reluctance. That ſweet girl bathed me in the tears of innocence and affection—ſhe told me, "that the fear leſt his preſence ſhould incenſe Lord Arlington to further brutality, had induced Eſſex, when I loſt my ſenſes, to withdraw from a ſcene which rent his very heart—and the ſame reaſon ſtill obliged him to remain at a diſtance.—That during the long and dire uncertainty attending my illneſs, he had ſcarcely breathed—his own ſoul continually told him how pure mine was. Fancy preſented me to him for ever, pale, ſpeechleſs, expiring; my ſad eyes rivetted on his with a tenderneſs death itſelf could not extinguiſh: however guiltleſs of my blood, every drop which oozed from my veins ſeemed to congeal on his heart; in fine, that almoſt deified by my ſufferings, and his ſenſe of them, I reigned alone in his affections, which were from this moment consecrated to me by a most convincing proof. Having used the utmost art and diligence to discover how Lord Arlington so soon became apprised of his secret return to England, and a meeting, so unplanned, and sudden, as to interrupt it almost immediately, though supposed to be as far off as Greenwich, Lord Essex learnt that his Master of the Horse, being among the domestics he brought with him to Pembroke House, had quitted it as soon as he alighted, and hastened to Greenwich in search of a girl attending on Lady Essex, of whom he was enamored; through whose means her Lady became likewise immediately acquainted with his secret arrival without knowing its motive. That suspicious woman had already remarked that Lord Arlington was among the bridal train, and in his hearing published the return of her Lord, with all her own injurious surmises—ill fortune for once had given them the color of truth, and Lord Arlington needed no more than the hint to make him mount the swiftest horse and ſly to ſatisfy himſelf.—Lady Eſſex was quickly informed of an incident ſhe ought to have foreſeèn, and giving way to another extravagance, paſſionately conjured every friend ſhe met to follow, and prevent the conflict to which her Lord now ſtood expoſed—but when could friendſhip keep pace with love and vengeance? The ſtraggling mediators arrived only time enough to witneſs the event no human power could guard againſt. Incenſed beyond all bounds at the conduct of his Lady, the raſh Eſſex took the only ſtep wanting to my ruin. Determined to make her ſhare the miſery ſhe had occaſioned, he parted with her at once and for ever---in vain were all her ſubſequent vows of ſorrow and repentance—in vain had ſhe from that moment indulged hopes of his cooling and conciliating—his temper, till this fatal period, no leſs yielding than fiery, now aſſumed a cold and philoſophic ſternneſs; in fine, that the grief and diſappointment to which Lady Eſſex reſigned herſelf would ſeverely puniſh her unjuſt ſuſpicions, and ere long releaſe her Lord from the ill-judged bondage he had hitherto groaned ſo impatiently under."

The fair Elizabeth thus ended her recital, which was ſo clear, conciſe, and affecting, that I could not avoid taxing her with being the emiſſary of her couſin; her bluſhes acquitted her, and beſpoke a ſecret time ſoon explained. She was ſecretly beloved by the gallant Southampton, that heroic friend who was only leſs attached to Eſſex than myſelf, and from him had learnt the various particulars public report could not appriſe her of.—I held myſelf infinitely indebted to her friendſhip, and through her means ſent that farewell to Lady Pembroke I was not allowed to pronounce.

It had been but too obvious through her whole recital, that I was totally the victim of calumny, nor could any human power now juſtify me.—I had been found in the arms of Eſſex---the fact was indubitable, the true cauſe of that fatal impulſe not likely to be credited, even when repeated.

peated. My youth, my wound, and my past conduct; blended the rash judgment of the many with compassion, but the most liberal-minded ventured not to acquit me. Those impassioned vindications the conscious soul of Essex offered, were always considered as a mere point of honor in him, and no less necessary to his own justification than mine; they therefore only served to stamp guilt on both— Oh, misjudging world, how severely on the most superficial observation dost thou venture to decide!---let the barbed arrow of misfortune rest in the bosom it has wounded, nor, by inhumanly tearing it out to discover whence it came, rack the heart already broken.

Defamed, dejected, and forgotten by all but the generous sisters of the Sydney family, I followed, once more, my fate in Lord Arlington; and reached again that Abbey destined alike to entomb me in playful childhood, and in blasted youth— the same imperious will which had destroyed me, had deprived the venerable mansion of its sweet, its solitary charms— the

the hallowed ſpot where once the ivied trophies of time bound up the defaced ones of religion, preſented nothing now but a bare and barren level; and the lofty woods, which ſo long protected alike the living and the dead, had wholly given place to infant plantations, through the thinneſs of which the weary eye every where pierced: I turned with diſguſt from the deſolated ſcene, and locking myſelf up in the remoteſt and moſt gloomy chambers of the Abbey, ſpent my life in meditating on my every loſs.

Lord Arlington now valuing me only as the appendage of his pride, conſoled himſelf for my undiſſembled averſion, and cared not what employed me, provided I was yet his legal priſoner.—Alas, I had no longer reſolution to reſt my hopes on any object—to form any ſubordinate deſign, or to reap any ſubordinate pleaſure. The poor children ſtill ſupported by my bounty, no more touched the lute in my preſence—that over which my own fingers once wandered with the wild elegance of untried youth,

now

now uselesſs and unſtrung, hung up, an emblem of the diſcordant ſoul of its owner. Taſte, genius, and ſcience, thoſe rich columns with which enthuſiaſtic fancy erects in peaceful minds a thouſand light aerial ſtructures, deep ſunk, and broken in my heart, preſented to the mental eye a ruin more terrible than the nobleſt ſpeculation ever pauſed over.—Miſanthropy, black-viſaged miſanthropy, reigned there like a ſolitary ſavage, unconſcious of the value of thoſe treaſures his rude hand every day more and more defaced.

I was rouſed one night with the information that a favourite ſervant of Lord Arlington's, who had long languiſhed in a conſumption, now found himſelf at the point of death, and importunately demanded to ſpeak with me—but ill-diſpoſed at this ſeaſon even to the gentle offices of humanity, and convinced that he could have nothing to impart I ſhould think of conſequence, I rejected the requeſt; but finding his Lord was inebriated beyond the power of comprehending

ing aught, on being again ſolicited, I roſe, and accompanied by a maid who loved me, entered the ſick man's chamber.—I caſt a harſh and cold glance round, and hardly heard the thanks he gave me—having diſmiſſed all the ſervants, except the maid I mentioned, I prepared to liſten to him, imagining ſome matter relative to his office of chief bailiff and ſurveyor, alone, could thus diſturb his laſt hours.—"Lady," ſaid he, in the hollow broken voice of approaching diſſolution, "I could not have departed in peace had you not beſtowed this indulgence—pardon me, I beſeech you, for propoſing to my Lord the deſtruction of thoſe ruins that I have ſince ſeen too plainly your heart was ever wrapt in—alas, the propoſal coſts me my life.—Condeſcend too to liſten to a ſecret which continually drags back my ſoul when ſtriving to quit her dungeon—my crime perhaps brings with it a ſufficient puniſhment.——In removing the rubbiſh of the artificial hermit's cell, in compliance with the directions of my Lord, I one day ſaw a common laborer turn up

ſomething

ſomething which tried his whole ſtrength, when caſting a quick and fearful glance around, he covered it with earth. I diſpatched the men in hearing to another part, and ſeizing the arm of him I had watched, I inſiſted on ſeeing what he had endeavoured to conceal—it proved to be a ſmall iron cheſt ſtrongly faſtened—I agreed with him to convey it away till the evening, when he might rejoin me, and we would open it and divide the contents together. He yielded rather to neceſſity than choice, and I took the caſket with a purpoſe God has ſeverely puniſhed—the many keys intruſted to my care ſupplied one which immediately opened it; under a number of papers and trifles of no value, I found a large ſum in gold, and a few jewels—as I knew my partner in the diſcovery had remarked that the cheſt was heavy; in the room of the gold and jewels, I ſubſtituted an iron crucifix and many ruſty keys; then locking the caſket, waited anxiouſly for the evening. The poor laborer ſeeing me return, wiſtfully examined my features, but

but not daring to expreſs the doubt viſible in his own, expected in ſilence the deciding hour. I ſuffered him to take infinite pains to break open a cheſt that I was conſcious would not repay the labor—great was the poor wretch's diſappointment when he emptied it—I affected the ſame chagrin; but turning over the papers, I offered to give him twenty nobles; a ſure proof, had he reflected a ſingle moment, that I muſt have wronged him: he readily accepted this propoſal, and, at my deſire, promiſed never to mention the incident; then with much apparent gratitude departed. Eagerly I replaced my guilty gains, and ſecretly reſolved to take an early opportunity of quitting my Lord to commence builder in London; but fear did not ſuffer me for a time to venture this meaſure; alas! I have wanted health ſince to do any thing—from this moment, peace, appetite, and reſt have fled me—if worn out with watching, I dropt into a ſlumber, the idea that my treaſure was ſtolen has made me often ſtart up, and regardleſs of the cold ſweat

pro-

produced by the mere apprehenſion, I have flown in the dead of night to convince myſelf it was ſafe—imaginary whiſpers have ever been near my bed, and uncertain forms have glided through my chamber—the dawn of day never gave me relief, every eye ſeemed to dive into my ſecret, and every hand to be intent on impoveriſhing me—in a word, Lady, to this ſad moment it has prematurely brought me; for many months doubtful whether I ſhould ſurvive, I have been conſidering how to beſtow that wealth I could no longer hope to enjoy—the poor man I ſo baſely defrauded of it periſhed a ſhort time after by the fall of a pillar, and reſtitution to him can never be made. It came into my head this evening, that you were ſaid to have been brought up in theſe ruins; certainly I had often ſeen you walk and weep on the very ſpot where this cheſt was found; perhaps therefore in giving it to you I only reſtore it to the right owner; accept it, Madam, and promiſe that you will never diſcover the gift to my Lord."——This requeſt appeared a

needleſs

needlefs injunction, if the treafure had not been obtained by defrauding Lord Arlington; and though perhaps I fhould have been filent through choice, I thought it beneath me to engage to be fo:—finding me paufe, he continued, "fear not any ill defign in this requeft, Madam, you will one day be glad you complied with it, and for your own fake alone is it propofed; the hand of my Lord is grudging—yours bounteous as that of heaven.—Do not rob yourfelf of the means to be liberal which now are offered to you—yet on no other condition than the vow of filence will I give the treafure up." A ftrange defire to examine the papers more than any I felt for the money, made me at laft acquiefce. My maid, by his direction, drew the iron cheft from an obfcure corner, and emptied it of both gold, jewels, and papers, which fhe and I divided, and with fome difficulty concealed till we reached my apartment—he feemed only to have lived to make this difcovery, and a few hours after expiated his fin with his life.

While

While he ſtrove to impreſs my mind with the neceſſity of concealing the adventure, I pondered deeply over it; not eaſily diſcerning how I ſhould interpret this ſtrange ordination of providence; it at laſt occurred to me that the treaſure might be put into my hands for the aſſiſtance and comfort of my ſiſter:—how did I know whether ſhe was not even then haſtening towards me, perhaps impoveriſhed, certainly diſtreſſed?—Oh, how conſolatory ſhould I find it to miniſter to her external wants, though thoſe of her heart might be beyond my power of comforting! The contempt I felt for Lord Arlington was rooted too deep to admit of my thus applying his fortune, had I been the unlimited miſtreſs of it; I therefore ſaw a degree of wiſdom and propriety in receiving and ſecreting a gift, heaven ſeemed ſo ſtrangely to put into my hands, as if it were to forerun ſome yet unknown incident.

The papers conſiſted chiefly of the correſpondence between Mrs. Marlow and

Father Anthony, while yet they were lovers, as well as after the cruel discovery which annulled the nominal union—I perused these invaluable epistles with pulsations of tenderness I lately thought myself incapable of; they recalled me to life and sensibility, and I gathered fortitude from those who now were dust; I raised my eyes to heaven in search of their pure translated souls, and wandering from planet to planet, fancied there must be one peculiarly allotted to lovers now no longer unhappy—A thousand trifles whose value must ever be ideal and local, were preserved with these letters:—cyphers, hair, sonnets, dear perpetuators of those bright hours of youth we look back on with pleasure to the latest moment of decaying life. I kissed the innocent reliques of such an unhappy attachment with devout regard, and held them not the least part of my legacy.

Time dissipated the flattering illusion which led me to expect my sister—my mind sunk into its usual inertitude, and

and the acquiſition remained, if not forgotten, at leaſt neglected.

From this profound ſtupor I was at laſt rouſed as by an earthquake—Lord Arlington in hunting fell from his horſe, and breaking ſome blood-veſſel, was brought home to appearance lifeleſs—conſcience and humanity called upon me to forget my wrongs; and I made every effort to ſave him: for a time he appeared to mend; but the incurable habit of inebriety he even at this period indulged, defeated both care and medicine; and after enduring a ſeries of ſufferings which annihilated my ſenſe of injury, he expired in the prime of his days.

Good heaven! what a tranſition did one ſingle event make in my life!—habituated to ſlavery—accuſtomed to ſuppoſe Lord Arlington deſtined to ſurvive me, I beheld this incredible revolution with mute ſurpriſe.... the horror of his ſufferings gave way, when they ceaſed, to the ſweet idea of liberty—liberty ſighed out my weary heart, ah! to what purpoſe have I now acquired it? I beheld myſelf in the ſituation of a criminal, whoſe ſhackles are ſtruck off only to launch him into the immenſe ocean in a little boat without a rudder, oars, or ſuſtenance—where could I find a hope to reſt on? alone, in the vaſt univerſe, I turned around in vain in ſearch of one generous hand, whoſe aid I might receive without fear or ſhame.

The relation of Lord Arlington who ſucceeded to his title and eſtate, was an illiterate rude ſea officer, whom his illneſs alone had detained in England. He came on the news of his deceaſe; eſcorting the late Lord's two ſiſters, to whom the perſonals were all deviſed. I had waited only the reading of the will to quit the melancholy manſion I meant to abjure for the future.—Gracious heaven! how deep was my indignation and rage to find myſelf mentioned in it as an inſane wretch, to whom the teſtator bequeathed a mere maintenance, and left to be confined under the charge of his ſiſters in St. Vincent's Abbey, which, as a purchaſe of his own,

de-

descended to them! Never, in all the trials I had hitherto experienced, had I felt a transport like that this usage excited—to extend his tyranny beyond the grave!—Mean, execrable wretch! even at the moment that I was exhausting the little constitution his cruelty had left me in unwearied attendance, deliberately to condemn me to an imprisonment so shocking, and render it perpetual!—human nature could not resist so pungent a pang—it *made* the misery it punished; and I sunk into the dreary gulph once more from which I was lately emerging—my brain still fires but to remember it.—Oh, my sister! whatever the inflictions of your mysterious fate, those of mine may surely dispute the woful pre-eminence.

The overjoyed Essex dispatched an express, as soon as the news of Lord Arlington's death reached the Court, conjuring me to quit the melancholy prison I had so long inhabited, and retire to a ſeat of Lord Southampton, in Herefordſhire; whither that nobleman's bride would immediately repair to meet and comfort me. Lady Southampton was the fair couſin of Lord Eſſex I formerly mentioned, who by marrying privately had wholly loſt the favor of the Queen. The declining ſtate of Lady Eſſex's health, he added, daily promiſed him that freedom, made doubly deſirable now I had recovered mine. It had always, he aſſured me, been the intention of Lady Southampton to follow her Lord to Ireland; and he beſought me to give him the ſweet ſatisfaction of knowing that I was ſafe in the company and protection of his couſin, ſolemnly promiſing not to obtrude himſelf on me ere the laws of ſociety authorized the avowal of thoſe ſentiments which had ſo long lived in his heart.

The relations of Lord Arlington, poſſeſſing by his will an abſolute power, intercepted and opened this Letter—far from pouring the balm it contained into my bleeding heart, they kept the dear teſtimony of an unequalled attachment; and ſent back the meſſenger with the melancholy news of my inſanity and confinement: but Lord Eſſex had been already duped, and could not eaſily credit this information. He deputed Henry Tracey, a young officer, much in his confidence, to aſcertain my real ſituation, commanding him not to be diſmiſſed by any other mode of conviction than that of being admitted into my preſence.—Alas! ere this was reſolved on, reſentment had again filled my bewildered brain, and Lord Arlington had little to apprehend in allowing Tracey to enter my apartment. Buried in a profound ſtupor, I replied not to his queſtions, but drawing my mourning veil over my eyes, ſat like a ſelf-devoted Perſian, the voluntary victim of deſpair. The faithful Tracey, ſtill fearful of being impoſed on, inſiſted on having my picture, as well as a lock of my hair, to prove to his Lord that it was indeed *myſelf* he had beheld in this deplorable ſtate; and having obtained this requeſt, he departed.

But what became of Eſſex when Tracey returned with this melancholy confirmation?—the teſtimonials his confidant had brought only added force to the eternal paſſion of his ſoul; a thouſand times he made Tracey deſcribe the apartment—my dreſs—my looks—and ſometimes fancying even that cautious friend had been deceived; at others, that the wretches in whoſe power I was left, had, for the ſhort period Tracey was permitted to behold me, ſtupified my ſenſes; he created a thouſand deluſions to counteract the fearful impreſſion of the truth.

Diſtracted with theſe ideas, Lord Eſſex ſet out for Ireland, inveſted with abſolute powers, and heading an army attached to him alike by gratitude and expectation—he had not marched far ere he formed the bold reſolution of committing the conduct of the troops to Lord Southampton, and turning off he haſtened to St. Vincent's Abbey, determined to judge from his own ſenſes of the ſtate of mine: he arrived there at midnight, and requiring the

the unwilling owners to produce me, in a tone which admitted neither denial or delay, they conducted him to my chamber—a dim lamp alone glimmered in it, and closing my eyes as the stronger lights approached, I waved my hand in stupid silence to have them removed. The transports of grief and surprise which overcame the generous Essex at this terrible conviction, threatened his own intellects—by some wonderful ordination of providence, my cold and apparently uninformed heart waked at that well-known voice—day broke once more upon my soul, and my eyes once more opened to behold their darling object. This surprising effect of his presence would have persuaded him that reason had never deserted me, but that my poor maids expressed a joy at this unexpected revolution too unfeigned to be misconstrued; they entreated him to leave me time to strengthen my faculties ere he again absorbed them, and he confined to

stifled

ſtifled exclamations, and ſilent homage; all the paſſion and projects with which his boſom ſwelled.

Alithea, who had for years been my favorite attendant, informed him (as ſoon as he could be perſuaded to withdraw, and leave me to repoſe) of the cruel and unjuſt will, which by rendering me a priſoner for life, had occaſioned this dreadful relapſe. Negligent at all times of prudence, and now perhaps of propriety, he boldly told the Arlington family, that he would periſh ere I ſhould again be left in their power; and having planted ſome of his moſt faithful domeſtics to guard my chamber door from every one but my own maids, he retired to the apartment allotted him, to meditate on the mode of proceeding leaſt likely to endanger my newly recovered intellects.

Alithea very prudently had me bled, and I ſunk into a ſweet and ſound ſleep, the comfort I had long moſt wanted. I waked late the next morning with intellects entirely clear, though weak; I remembered I had ſeen, or fancied I had ſeen Eſſex; Althea imparted to me the truth, and ſhed tears of joy to find I anſwered her rationally—I yielded to her intreaties in delaying till the afternoon a meeting ſo dear and affecting, and took the medicinal cordials and other nouriſhment ſhe offered me; a few hours ſtrengthened me ſurpriſingly, and I was at laſt allowed to receive the generous lover my ſoul ſo much deſired. While he poured forth the moſt ardent vows of unremitting affection, and ſurveyed, in tender ſorrow, the ravages grief and diſappointment had thus early made in my wan countenance, and emaciated form, I beheld with ſurpriſe the advantages he had acquired in both inſtances; his graceful flower of youth was ſettled into firmer manhood; his fair and florid complexion, ſunned over by his military exploits, had gained ſtrength without loſing delicacy, and his eye, now no leſs accuſtomed to command than charm, ſeemed to employ its firſt power on all the reſt of the world, while its laſt was ſolely reſerved for me. Ah man, happy man! how ſuperior are you in the indulgence of nature! bleſt with ſcientific reſources, with boldneſs, and an activity unknown to more perſecuted woman; from your various diſappointments in life ever ſpring forth ſome vigorous and blooming hope, inſenſibly ſtaunching thoſe wounds in the heart through which the vital powers of the feebler ſex bleed helpleſsly away; and when relenting fortune grants your wiſhes, with unblighted powers of enjoyment you embrace the dear-bought happineſs; ſcarce conſcious of the cold dew-drops your cheeks imbibe from thoſe of her, permitted too late to participate your deſtiny.

It was ſome days ere I dared truſt myſelf to converſe long with Eſſex, who employed that ſweet interval in amuſing my mind with lighter topics, while he arranged his future plans; but finding I ſtill appeared calm, he ventured at laſt to unfold to me the mighty deſigns which floated in his imagination. "Inexorably oppoſing choice to fate, my deareſt Ellinor,"

nor," ſaid he, " never from the moment in which I firſt beheld you, have I formed a project diſtinct from yourſelf; this I am about to unfold has been for years the child of my dotage—collect your ſpirits, liſten without wonder, and, if poſſible, approve it: from the moment I knew the baſe arts that muſt have been made uſe of to ſeparate us, I clearly comprehended that we ſhould never unite with the conſent of Elizabeth; but, however indebted to her partial diſtinction, this was a point in which even ſhe could not controul me; it is not the poſts or advantages I derive from her favor, on which my ſoul values itſelf; elevated on a more ſolid foundation, it has taken every road to glory, and I may proudly ſay, given a grace to dotage: yet as that dotage, however unbecoming her years and her rank, has been uniform and generous, I have ſworn to yield Elizabeth, to the lateſt moment of her life, every homage but that of the heart; and ſacrifice to my fealty all except my happineſs.—It is hard to reconcile duties

and

and inclinations ſo entirely oppoſite, yet I think you will own I have done ſo.

To a blind partiality for me, and her own egregious ſelf-love, the Queen ignobly ſacrificed your youth, your hopes, your happineſs; but alas, ſhe forgot in ſo doing, that ſhe would only make them more perfectly mine—without the leaſt conſideration for the huſband ſhe had given you, a wretch I could at any time look into inſignificance, I ſtudied ſolely how to extricate you from a bondage not more inſupportable to you than myſelf.—Among a thouſand other projects, I reſolved to apprize the king of Scots of your exiſtence and ſituation, ſoliciting from his fraternal regard a ſafe aſylum, and that peace and protection my youth and circumſtances would not allow me to offer you. I found means to convey to his knowledge your whole melancholy ſtory—but how ſhall I declare to you his ungenerous conduct? Fool that I was, to hope the man who could tamely ſubmit to the murder of his mother, would be intereſted by any other tye! Far from exerting himſelf to reſcue the dear unhappy ſiſter I conjured him to compaſſionate, he affected to diſbelieve the ſtory of his mother's marriage with the Duke of Norfolk; though the Counteſs of Shrewſbury ſolemnly aſſured me that he had, through her hands, received from the Royal Mary the moſt authentic proofs of it, as ſoon as he eſcaped from the power of the Regent, and was allowed to act as an independent Sovereign. Anxious without doubt to centre in himſelf every right of his mother, he voluntarily renounced all regard for either her aſhes or her offſpring, ignominiouſly ſubmitting to kiſs the hand which had ſhortened her days.——What after this is to be hoped from the king of Scots? and why ſhould you ſacrifice to a brother, by whom you are diſowned, thoſe bright proſpects which now dawn before you? Born of the firſt Engliſh Peer, and the Princeſs immediate in ſucceſſion to the Throne—a native of this kingdom; there is only one thing wanting to eſtabliſh rights from whence you may juſtly form the higheſt hopes—

authentic

authentic teſtimonials of theſe facts; and that ſuch ſtill exiſt, I have certain information—it is true they are diſperſed ſolely among the Catholic relations and friends of Mary, yet do I not deſpair of obtaining them.——The Engliſh, ever diſpoſed to be jealous of their national rights, dread the remoteſt chance of their annihilation, and already turn their eyes towards the family of Suffolk in preference to receiving a foreign monarch.—That unhappy family, by turns the martyrs of fear and policy, has bled through ſucceeding generations, till reduced wholly to females; among whom there is not one endued with courage or talents to venture a conteſt, had they even the priority of birth which reſts with you. Let us then adopt the views of Lord Leiceſter, who certainly meant, by the moſt watchful policy, to pave the way for your ſiſter's ſucceſſion, whenever Elizabeth ſhould expire. Your fate is bound up with that of a man much more capable of effecting whatever views he ſhall adopt.

Eli-

Elizabeth daily totters on the verge of the grave—disposed to hate the Prince she has irretrievably injured in the person of his mother, she still refuses to acknowledge the King of Scots for her heir; and has fully invested me with every power that may enable me to profit by the popularity I have honorably acquired. My own birth, though it does not give me a lineal claim to the Crown of England, is yet noble in many generations, and princely in some. Circumstances and merit thus entitle me to match with you—nor need you doubt the success of this project.—Born as you are for empire, endued with beauty to adorn, and majesty to dignify it—with incontestable evidence of your birth (which I will employ every art to procure) I will boldly present to the people of England another blooming Queen—they will with joy adopt you; nor can the feeble attempts of the boyish Scotch pedant against an army won by my munificence, endeared to my command, and relying on my valor, affect a claim ſo ſtrongly ſupported. How many inſtances does our own hiſtory ſupply where courage and popularity have dethroned monarchs in full poſſeſſion of every other advantage!—You now are informed of what has long been the ultimate object of my life; every action and view has had a ſecret reference to it, and far from idling away my youth in the various pleaſures the gay court of Elizabeth offered to her favorite, I have continually ranged the ſeas, watched in camps, diſciplined armies, and by every poſſible means ſtudied to increaſe my military fame, knowledge, and popularity, as what muſt one day decide more than my own fate. It is this that has made me eager to conduct the Iriſh war—In that country I ſhall be at the head of an army, which will eaſily enable me to profit by the death of the Queen, without alarming her declining years with the appearance of cabal, myſtery, or rebellion.---Boldly reſolve then, my love, to accompany me to Ireland, as the only place on earth where you can be entirely ſafe; I will lodge you in ſome impregnable fortreſs with Lady Southampton; I will remain in the camp, and never approach it but by your permiſſion---I demand this inſtance of your confidence, of your love; and ſwear in return inviolable honor and obedience—Oh! anſwer me not raſhly, ſweet Ellinor—rather recall the fatal moment of obſtinate prudence which once before brought on both ſo tedious a period of ſuffering, and remember you again have the power of deciding my fate and your own.

Eſſex roſe from my feet, and left me buried in the deepeſt reflection; my mind, however, inſtantaneouſly adopted the aſpiring project he had preſented to it. Through the dark and heavy cloud which had long hung over my ſoul, the ſun of love now pierced at once, and turned it all to ambient gold.---To mount a throne, to ſhare it with the choice of my heart; to give to him that ſovereignty I ſhould owe to his valor---I was aſtoniſhed that the idea could ſo long have eſcaped me: yet ſuch a train of misfortunes had ſucceeded my birth, as might well obliterate my ſenſe of its rights. "Baſe and unworthy ſon!" ſighed I, "ungenerous, cruel brother! why ſhould I ſacrifice to thee my only chance on this ſide the grave?" The mean acquieſcence of James, under a blow which almoſt nerved my arm againſt the royal murderer, had already ſufficiently ſhocked my feelings, and ſhut him out of all my plans; alas, I could only excuſe his miſconduct by ſuppoſing that he was yet ſubjected to his mother's enemies, though even then, a generous ſoul would reſolutely have proteſted againſt the evil it could not prevent; but to be aſſured that he ſacrificed an inviolable duty, and every ſocial feeling at the ſhrine of that bloated idol, *ſelf*, robbed him of all claim to the feelings, the duties, he renounced. The determined plan of the generous Eſſex had every thing in its favor, nor was my concurrence ſo neceſſary to his ſucceſs as happineſs—but wherefore ſhould I heſitate,

ſitate, when not to unite in it was to deliver myſelf up to an implacable enemy? yet, as avowedly to depart with Eſſex, or even after him, would awaken dangerous ſuſpicions in the mind of Elizabeth, and confirm all the ſlanders of the world; I pondered much on a ſingular idea that aroſe in my mind, by which both might be obviated; indeed the ſituation of my health would have ſufficiently oppoſed my going with him, had no other objection occurred.---I perceived an air of ſtifled anger in Eſſex when he returned, which I conjured him to expound:---"It is a matter of no conſequence," ſaid he, with his uſual frankneſs; "fortunately the few friends I have brought with me are tried and valiant, and we have the power in our own hands: the wretches, my love, who ſurround you, pretend an authority from the Queen, as well as from the late Lord Arlington, for your detention; this will oblige us to uſe a violence I would rather have avoided; but that is a trifle." "Oh! call not any thing a trifle which affects your ſafety, however remotely," cried I; "in yielding to the bold project you have ventured to form, beware I do not become its ruin---yes, look not on me with so marked a wonder; my soul accords to, adopts at once all your views. I will at last indulge my heart, and thus affiance it to yours---born to pursue your fortune, I will joyfully consent to partake it, so you, in return, swear the confidence will render you but more guarded; in considering my own honor, I am only watching over yours; pledge then your word that you will not interfere with my plan, and I in return will vow, that all I henceforward form, shall have the same tendency with your own."

The generous Essex scarce credited his senses, and gave with readiness the assurance I desired.---Resolved to guard my sister's prior rights, and unable to judge of the motives which might bury her for a time in oblivion, I insisted on his supporting her claim in preference to mine, if ever she should appear; and he perhaps the more readily acquiesced in this request, from a conviction that she no longer

longer exiſted, as all my opinions on that head appeared to him entirely viſionary.

Refuſing to confide in this dear raſh lover the means by which I meant to rejoin him, I obliged him to aſſume an air of grief and deſpair, which perſuaded the Arlington family that I had relapſed into inſanity. In the interim a maid of mine had been ſeized with an epidemic fever of the moſt dangerous kind; I impatiently haſtened the departure of Eſſex, leſt the cruel malady ſhould infect him, and conjured him to wait with Lady Southampton at the port, from whence the troops had already embarked, till I ſhould rejoin him. The air of ſatisfaction he perceived in me made him comply againſt his better judgment, and the Arlington race, no leſs overjoyed at his departure than my ſuppoſed relapſe, and fearful of the epidemic fever, ſhut up thoſe who immediately attended on me, in the quarter of the Abbey I inhabited, avoiding it themſelves as though the plague were encloſed there.

In this solitude I executed a surprising project I had long meditated: from the moment I was informed of the mock interment of Lord Leicester, my mind had dwelt on the idea; I saw it was only to methodize the most wild and romantic plan, and, however unfeasible it at first appeared, time might form and bring it to effect—The treasure of the surveyor now became a treasure indeed, reflection convinced me that the bequest originated in his having been the confidant as well as witness of his Lord's ungenerous will, and by thus disposing of his own acquisition, he enabled me to escape from the despicable bondage it entailed upon me, without betraying his trust.---The maid, who alone witnessed the mysterious legacy, had, by her inviolable silence on so singular an event, sufficiently proved that she could merit my whole confidence; fortunately, she was no less favored by those in whose power I was left, and became of course the properest, and only assistant I could fix on.---by thus turning the artifice of the Queen upon herself, I might at once escape from

her

her power, and that of the guardians under whofe care fhe had placed me; and gratify the firft wifh of Effex without endangering his fafety.

Alithea embraced the plan with joy, and engaged her parents, who were laborers in the neighbourhood, to aid the delufion.---I affected to be feized with the fame fatal fever as foon as the maid's fymptoms became mortal, and when fhe foon after died, refigned my bed to her corpfe: her hair, height, complexion, and age, fo far agreed with mine as to fecure me from common obfervation, and dread of the contagion faved us from a very ftrict fcrutiny. as it was believed that the maid expired nearly at the fame time with myfelf, by Alithea's judicious management her fuppofed body was to be delivered to the parents of that faithful domeftic; when placing myfelf and treafure in the homely coffin, I was boldly conveyed like the Emprefs Maud through the midft of my enemies, and lodged in their humble cot, till enough recovered to purfue the route of Effex.

Alithea now publiſhed the news of my death through the family, who heard of it with joy; the unguarded conduct of the generous Eſſex had ſuggeſted to them, that to have acted under the authority of the Queen, might one day be a very inſufficient vindication:---this idea added fear to that hatred they always entertained for me, and with pleaſure they buried both thoſe paſſions in my grave.---Having ſurveyed my wardrobe, jewels, and papers, without finding the leaſt deficiency, they prepared for my interment, and diſcharged my immediate attendants; among them the favored one who had aided my ſcheme, and her return to her parents reſtored peace to my boſom.

From the humble cot of that honeſt creature's parents do I cloſe this period of my memoirs---here, as from an inviſible world, have I ſurveyed the gloomy pageant, with which the erroneous judgments of thoſe from whom I eſcaped have dignified a low-born female, and by placing her pompouſly at the ſide of Lord Arlington, they perhaps have blundered uncon-

unconſciouſly on propriety.---As the ſable train wound by my window, my ſoul pauſed on the ſolemn vanity———Oh! that in thy tomb, thou quiet ſleeper, ſighed I, may be interred with my name all the painful part of my exiſtence! that renovated to a new and happier being, I may emerge again into a world which ſtill opens a flowery path before me, with corrected ſpirits, unfaltering reaſon, and a temper ſuperior to the ſhocks of misfortune!——

* * * * * *

The ſoul, ever capricious and uncertain, fully enjoys only the pleaſures it makes for itſelf.---Often do I ſeem even in this ruſtic aſylum, concealed in the coarſe garments of the other ſex, and looking towards a diſtant kingdom as my home, to have hoards of hope and happineſs to build on, my youthful, healthful days were never bleſt with.——

* * * * * *

My

My own fate has once more recalled to my mind that of Matilda—I have meditated much on a ſiſter ſo dear—alas, too certainly Eſſex is in the right, and there exiſts not a being I can call by that name.—Long years have ſucceeded each other, and ſtill that incomprehenſible myſtery, that dreadful ſilence continues; nor is there a circumſtance but death that could occaſion it.—Farewell then, oh name ever ſo pleaſant to my lips, ſink deep into my heart, and remain eternally engraved there—farewell, thou pure ſpirit! too ethereal for a world ſo groſs, I will no more look for thee on its ſurface, I will no more imagine thee beneath it—no, I will now raiſe my ſteadfaſt eye to that heaven "where the wicked ceaſe from troubling," and in ſome yet undiſcovered ſtar fancy I behold thee! Ah deign, if ſo, to guide the uncertain ſteps of a wanderer, and, if my cruel fate conduct them ſtill toward precipices, irradiate the ſcene, and deliver me from the danger!—My ſpirits are highly wrought, and a ſolemnity too exquiſite for deſcription poſſeſſes

every

every faculty—I muſt ſteep them all in oblivion ere I recover my equanimity.——

* * * * * *

Happineſs! undefinable good, in what ſhall I compriſe thee? no, I will not ſuppoſe it can be done in gold, and yet how pure was the tranſport a little of that vile metal called into the care-furrowed countenances of Alithea's venerable parents! To the earth which gave, I have reſtored the remainder; it is buried eaſtward under the ſpreading cheſnut planted by Edward IV.—that popular tree, protected alike from the caprice of its owner, and the ſpade of the laborer, will hide it ſafely: but, oh! if ever one noble heart ſighs under its ſhade, oppreſſed with the ſting of penury, may ſome good angel whiſper, "you reſt on that which can fully relieve you."

All is now prepared for my flight; I have refuſed the attendance of Alithea; it will be well ſupplied in the remembrance

brance that ſhe is happy—indulgent heaven has given to *her* parents who grow old in peace and virtue, a lover who knows not falſehood or ambition, and a ſoul juſtly grateful for bleſſings beyond all valuation—the faithful creature delays the happineſs of him ſhe loves till he ſhall have conveyed this broken narrative into the hands of Lady Pembroke; nor do I fear to truſt him with it.—Dear, noble friend, once more my ſoul fondly ſalutes you; beſtow on my flight thoſe pious prayers with which virtue conſecrates our purpoſes, and believe mine riſe ever for you.

LADY PEMBROKE WRITES.

Hardly had I recovered from the ſurpriſe and grief occaſioned by the publication of this ſweet creature's ſuppoſitious death, ere a ruſtic demanded permiſſion to ſee me, and myſteriouſly delivered the wonderful packet—alas, how affecting did I find it!

far, however, from drying up my tears at learning the angel yet lived, I looked with terror on the future, left every following day should multiply, or terribly finish her miseries. Ah, dear Matilda! I cannot agree with this fair visionary, who so easily adopts the romance of her lover.—Something seems to assure me thou art still alive, and suffering; and for thy sake I will preserve these melancholy memorials: alas! perhaps it were more generous to destroy them.

LETTER I.

Dated Drogheda.

FROM the safe shores of another kingdom once more do I greet my friend.—Alas! ill can we judge for ourselves, dear Lady Pembroke.

Provided with a fleet horse, I set out to follow Essex, but scarce had I travelled a single day, ere my shattered constitution (no longer able to sustain the least toil) claimed two, to recover the fatigue of the first. During my stay at the inn, my youth,

youth, the delicacy of my perſon and manners, with the air of reſerve I found it neceſſary to aſſume, excited a curioſity my liberality alone was able to bound, though even that gave riſe to ſuſpicions almoſt equally dangerous. I began to fear that my ſcheme would wholly fail in the execution; I hired, however, two ruſtics, well recommended, as a guide, and an eſcort, yet in travelling on the ſolitary mountains of Wales, often dared not turn my head over my ſhoulder, leſt in my guards I ſhould behold my murderers. My impaired health rendered the journey very tedious; during its progreſs, I paſſed for a poor youth following the ſteps of my father, and far gone in a conſumption—After immenſe fatigue, I arrived at length at the port; where I underſtood with inexpreſſible chagrin that Eſſex had embarked for Ireland a week before.---Alas! a moment's recollection enabled me to account for this, apparently, ſtrange deſertion:---in my eagerneſs to conceal my favorite ſcheme, I had forgotten to guard againſt

against the chance of his being informed of my supposed death ere I reached him. On inquiry, I plainly perceived that he had left spies in the neighbourhood of St. Vincent's Abbey when he quitted it, who, misled by report, had hastened after him with news of the melancholy event. I learnt that he had delayed crossing from time to time without giving any reason for it, but on being roused by the arrival of two officers, he ordered the seamen to be called in the dead of night, and embarked the moment the tide favoured his departure.

Though this information left me only myself to reproach, it did not lessen my chagrin. I wandered toward the shore to meditate at leisure; it was still littered with soldiers and their appendages: they were indulging with ungoverned licence in drinking and riot.—Every thing I beheld, increased my fears of the voyage; it was indeed a tremendous project, to embark with a numerous body of licentious men for an unknown country, while wrapt in mystery myſelf, and without a protector.—How if actuated by curioſity, or a leſs excuſable motive, they ſhould gueſs at my ſex, and pry into my ſtory? Perhaps even the name of their general would want influence to guard me. I turned woman again, and trembled at the bare idea. While irreſolute in what manner to diſpoſe of my unfortunate ſelf, I obſerved a body of travellers approaching, and underſtood with joy that it was Lady Southampton and her train, eſcorted by a choſen troop, for whom thoſe I had already ſeen waited.—I bleſt indulgent heaven, which thus relieved me from the effects of my own indiſcretion, and demanded to ſee her---to ſee her was enough, for with the penetration natural to her ſex, ſhe inſtantly knew me, and throwing her arms around my neck, reproached me with a generous freedom for having retarded her journey, by obliging her to wait in vain for my arrival: and finally, for ſhocking her with the fictitious ſtory of my death.---I explained to her my unguarded conduct, and its motives---She aſſured me that ſhe dreaded the effect it might have on my lover, as her Lord had not time to write more than that Eſſex was in deſpair for my loſs, nor dared he venture to leave him; therefore conjured her to confide herſelf to the care of the officers he mentioned, and follow with all expedition.---This information doubled the regret which had already ſeized on me; but to guard againſt all ſuſpicion and inquiry, I reſolved to retain my maſculine habit, and paſs for one of Lady Southampton's pages, till ſafely lodged in Ireland.

We arrived here laſt night, and found a letter from Lord Southampton, lamenting the impoſſibility of waiting for his Lady, without abandoning Eſſex to a grief which urged him to raſhneſs and deſpair; he ended with conjuring her to remain in this town till he had conſidered how to diſpoſe of her ſafely.—Oh, fortune, fortune, how unfairly do we accuſe thee, when folly alone has led us into error! I am more miſerable than it is poſſible to exprefs. Lady Southampton would fain perfuade me that this overfight may eventually prove lucky, as it will prevent my again feeing Effex ere the death of his Lady.—Ah! what alteration can her lofs make in my fate?—"I tell you, my watchful friend, you cannot love my honor more than I do his fafety—between him and me there is another bar not lefs infurmountable.—Did not my fifter's marriage with a favorite of Elizabeth coft him his life? Alas, perhaps hers too was facrificed!"—Over her myfterious fate a dark veil early fell, dipt perhaps in the blood of her beloved—rather may I fee my own veins opened, than furvive fuch a calamity; but even at this moment it has perhaps fallen on me, and I may be dying in Effex while yet unconfcious of my fate—oh, what horrors take poffeffion of my foul at the bare idea!———Lady Southampton has fealed her Englifh difpatches, and I can only fay adieu.

LETTER II.

Dated Drogheda.

BOUND to this ſpot, my generous friend, and dreading all which paſſes beyond it, hardly can my heart feel the congratulation you beſtow. Environed by enemies, and rendered raſh by deſpair, Eſſex now renounces the glorious viſions he poſſeſſed my imagination with, and reſigns himſelf wholly up to his command.—Oh, that the arrow which ſtabs me ſhould have been ſharpened by my own hand!—All here is alarm, uncertainty, and confuſion—we get and loſe in the courſe of every day a paſſage to our friends, nor dare we truſt to that channel aught of importance. Sir Coniers Clifford with a choſen body of troops was yeſterday ſurrounded, himſelf and half his men cut off immediately—among the officers was a relation of Lady Southampton's; ſhe has been weeping the whole day for him.—For my own part, conſcious that I have not a tear to ſpare for common inflictions, I gather mine into my heart, which feels ready to pour forth a deluge the moment one of my many fears ſhall be confirmed.—You can form no conception of the wants, the woes, the horrible ſcenes we witneſs.—Born and bred in the arms of luxury and proſperity, a diſtant war but faintly affects our minds; but oh, how tremendous does it appear when once we are driven into its tempeſtuous ſeat!—death, ghaſtly death, aſſumes a bloody variety of forms; while rapine, famine, ſickneſs, and poverty, fearfully forerun him.

I have hitherto thought my ſiſter's fate more conſummately wretched than even my own, but how is every evil lightened by compariſon!—Beloved Matilda, born as you were to woe, you ſaw but one bounded proſpect of the infinitude the globe preſents to us; the horrors of this were unknown to you—uncomforting is the pillow of her who ſleeps within the ſound of a drum, and fancies its every ſtroke is fate.—Is this to live? Ah no! it is to be continually dying.

This

This country ſo nearly allied to our own, yet offers to our view a kind of new world; divided into petty ſtates, inveterately hating each other, it knows not the benefit of ſociety, except when neceſſity combines the various parties againſt a common enemy; yet, though neceſſity unites, it cannot blend them; the leaſt ceſſation of general danger awakens all their narrow partialities and prejudices, which continually break out with bloody violence. The advantages of commerce, the charms of literature, all the graces of civilization, which at once enrich the mind, and form the manners, are almoſt unknown to this people; with a ſavage pride they fancy their very wants virtue, and owe to their poverty an unregulated valor, which often enables them to contend with well-diſciplined troops, whom they ſometimes defeat by mere want of knowledge; at others, on the contrary, they obſtinately purſue an unequal conteſt, while ſpeculating reaſon turns away from the bloody ſcene, vainly conſcious that their mingled bodies ſtrew the earth, only becauſe no benevolent being has yet deigned to attempt the conqueſt of their minds.

How deeply muſt ſuch reflections operate upon a heart bound up in the life of the accompliſhed leader! endued with but the common powers of humanity, expoſed with the reſt, alike to the ſword and to the elements, he, even he, muſt one day periſh; and while I weep the wretches every hour deprives of their beloved protectors, I know not but that I may at the ſame moment be added to the number.—Ah, if deſpair ſhould impel Eſſex,—his natural heroiſm needs no ſuch incentive,—ſhould he fall, unconſcious of my yet ſurviving, to that fatal though well deſigned artifice I ſhould for ever impute his loſs, and die for having feigned to do ſo.

A wild fancy has taken ſtrange poſſeſſion of my mind—Lady Southampton ſays it is madneſs; perhaps it really is ſo, but I can think of nothing elſe: ſhe, however is too timid to judge—ſhe will paſs her whole life here I really believe.

Were

Were I but for a moment to behold that expreſſive countenance,—were I by a kind of reſurrection again to appear before him!——

Something ſtrangely impels me—a choſen troop are now ſetting out.—I ſhall be ſafe under their protection.—Ah, if this ungovernable impulſe ſhould be but a preſentiment of his danger—never, never ſhould I forgive myſelf were I to leave him, wounded and dying, to the care of perſons comparatively indifferent.

"Argue no longer, my dear importunate friend, I will go, but depend on my haſtening back."—Lady Southampton would have made a wretched love for Eſſex; ſhe is the moſt apprehenſive of women; but ſhe was not born to mate with that aſpiring hero.

THE

RECESS, &c.

PART V.

A Silence ſo tedious will make you number me among the dead; recover yourſelf, my beloved friend—born to a perpetual conteſt with ill fortune, I ſink not even yet under the oppreſſion.—I have been collecting all my thoughts to purſue my ſtrange recital, more ſtrange indeed every day.

In

In our way towards Ulſter, we were intercepted by a body of the rebellious Iriſh, and a deſperate ſkirmiſh enſued.—How ſhall I own it, and call myſelf the love of Eſſex? yet ſo it was—I, who had been ſo valiant in imagination, and remote from the field of action—I, who had in fancy lifted a ſword with the ſtrength of Goliah, and interpoſed a ſhield before Eſſex, heavier perhaps than myſelf, ſhrunk into annihilation at the bare ſight of the conflict; and the faintings which laid me among the ſlain, perhaps alone ſaved me from being added to their number. I revived in the hands of ſome ferocious women, who in ſtripping the dead, had diſcovered at one moment that I yet lived, and was of their own ſex. Induced either by a ſentiment of humanity, or the hope of a reward, they liſtened to my eager ſupplications for life, and conveyed me to a neighbouring cabin; whither they ſummoned a prieſt, who opened a vein in my arm. On feebly

re-

reviving once more, I caſt my eyes round in ſpeechleſs aſtoniſhment, ſcarce knowing whether I ſhould think my eſcape a bleſſing. I was environed by a ſet of beings who in complexion alone bore any reſemblance to myſelf, their language, manners, and lives, ſeeming no more analogous, than thoſe of the inhabitants of the Torrid Zone. I laboured in vain to comprehend them, or to make myſelf underſtood, and was in deſpair giving up the attempt, when the prieſt already mentioned came to my relief. Through his means I informed them that the Lord Deputy would redeem me at any ranſom, provided they ſecured me from danger and inſult. I ſhould, I believe, have enſured my own ſafety, had not the victorious party learnt, by ſome ſtraggler, that an Engliſh woman of diſtinguiſhed rank had been diſcovered among the ſlain. They eagerly turned back to demand me, and the hope of reward alike influencing my preſervers to keep me in their hands, a diſpute no leſs fierce, though not ſo bloody,

bloody, as that I had before witneſſed, followed; it was too violent to be compromiſed, and at length, as the only way to prevent murder, both parties agreed that I ſhould be put into the hands of their General, Tiroen; or, as ſome called him, O'Neal. Intreaties or reſiſtance would have been equally vain, and I was obliged to rejoice that they thought me of conſequence enough to act ſo honourably by me.

During this interval, one of the ſervants deputed by Lady Southampton immediately to attend on me, having lingered a few minutes behind the Engliſh troop, followed to rejoin them at the moment of the onſet: the ſound of the firing reached him ere he fell in with the ſcouts, and clapping ſpurs to his horſe, he flew back to the village we all had lately quitted, there to wait in ſafety the event of the conteſt: at this place he was informed a band of rebels had iſſued out from an ambuſcade formed in the neighbouring mountain: and while he was wavering what ſtep to take, the

news

news of my ſex and capture ſuddenly reached him; ſtruck with the idea of ſome important myſtery, as well from my diſguiſe as the cautions of his Lady, he haſtened back to her with the ſtrange intelligence. The generous but timid Lady Southampton, impreſſed ſolely with the idea of my danger, wrote, inſtantaneouſly to Eſſex, briefly reciting all he did not know of my ſtory, and ſtrongly conjuring him to exert his utmoſt influence to preſerve me from danger or inſult.

But who ſhall paint the feelings of Eſſex, when this ſurpriſing intelligence firſt reached him! intelligence which, in one moment, opened all thoſe ſources of tenderneſs in his ſoul grief and deſpair had well nigh congealed. To think I ſtill lived would have been conſummate happineſs, had I not been thus unaccountably ſnatched away, even at the very moment of my miraculous renovation: ſo ſingular a complication of events almoſt deprived him of his ſenſes, and wrought impulſe up to agony. Perhaps the laſt untoward incident of my life was necessary to save his brain from partaking the distractions of his mind:—sick at the heart of an incurable sorrow—fatigued with the cares of government, and the slavery of command, the news of my existence and capture made him find in distinctions hitherto so oppressive, the sole prospect of recovering a treasure, which alone could give value to his future life.

From the knowledge acquired in his military command, Essex was enabled to decide on the character of Tiroen—he justly believed it unprincipled and ungovernable; how must he tremble then to recollect that my fate was in his hands! In a conjuncture so dangerous he resigned himself entirely up to the guidance of an impassioned heart, and dispatched an officer of rank, charging the arch-rebel, by the blood of thousands yet unspilt, not to exasperate the English, and himself in particular, by maltreating the lady fortune had thrown into his power; for whose ransom any sum

ſum was tendered her captors ſhould demand.

This raſh and impetuous addreſs had conſequences only leſs dangerous than thoſe it guarded againſt. Tiroen unfortunately diſcovered at once that he had the happineſs of the Lord Deputy in his keeping; and though he flattered him from time to time with promiſes of noble treatment, he ſecretly determined, no doubt, that if he ever parted with me, it ſhould be upon his own terms.

It was not till ſeveral of theſe meſſages had paſſed, that Tiroen's curioſity led him to pay me a viſit: the attention excited by my maſculine habit had led me immediately to requeſt one more ſuited to my ſex; and the delicate ſituation I ſtood in, obliging me to conduct myſelf with the utmoſt caution, I had thought it peculiarly fortunate to eſcape the notice of the General.

The continual repetition of his tedious viſits, when once he had ſeen me; the laviſh ſupply of ſuch accommodations as that

that ravaged country then afforded—an obstinate silence on the state of my affairs, and the most wearisome discussions of his own, all too soon convinced me that neither his pride, his ambition, or his ferocity, had been able to guard the heart of Tiroen from that powerful passion which invigorated the being of his distinguished rival—I trembled at recollecting that I was wholly in his power—already misjudged as the voluntary mistress of Essex, unwilling to announce myself, and unable, had I done so, to prove my right to distinction, mine was indeed a fearful situation. I was not allowed to hold any correspondence with the English, and only knew by the watch kept over me, that a human being was anxious for my release.

Whatever consequences might ensue from my appearing pleased with the distinctions lavished on me by Tiroen, I felt every day more sensibly that I had no other means of avoiding the licentious insolence of his officers; who fancied their services ſo important to the cauſe they had eſpouſed, as to ſecure their conduct from too ſtrict a ſcrutiny.

Tiroen meantime ſought occaſions to break off, renew, and prolong, the ſecret intercourſe in which he had now engaged with Eſſex; but a lingering treaty agreed not with the fiery impatience of that unfortunate hero. His divided ſoul no longer attended to the duties of his command—the buſineſs of the war was at an end—Eſſex was no longer a cool and prudent General, watchful to ſeize every advantage, and haraſs the enemy—alas, he was now only a wild and extravagant lover, ready to ſacrifice every conſideration to the recovery of one adored individual.—Delivered up to paſſion, to terror, to agony, to every torturing exceſs of overſtrained ſenſibility, at this fatal period the generous Eſſex was gradually ſacrificing the whole renown of a life hitherto ſo glorious. The news of Tiroen's love crowned his misfortunes; and that execrable traitor, determined to bring, if poſſible, the Lord Deputy to his terms, by various emiſſaries had him informed of plots he never laid againſt me, and repulſes he never ſuſtained; always ſpeciouſly diſowning ſuch deſigns, in terms calculated only to redouble the ſuſpicions of his rival.

By artifices like theſe the warlike talents and dignified mind of Eſſex were kept in abſolute ſubjection; he no longer dared to exert the valour which burned proudly at his heart, but ſtifling every emotion love did not excite, he eagerly engaged in a ſecret and dangerous treaty.—The raſh propoſal of Eſſex to confer with Tiroen from the oppoſite banks of a rivulet, I imputed to the paſſionate deſire a lover ever has to judge of the perſon and talents of the man who dares to rival him:—this interview could not be kept a ſecret—alas, perhaps it decided the fortune of the Lord Deputy.—Miſjudged from that moment by a buſy world which ſees only the ſurface of things, to timidity, to avarice, to indolence, to ambition, by turns, has been aſcribed an incident, of which love had all the merit or the ſhame.—Ah! had the erroneous multitude conſidered but a moment, ſurely they had diſcerned a myſtery in his conduct.—What could ambition, glory, pride, require, he did not poſſeſs already? If to hold the moſt abſolute ſway over the moſt abſolute of Sovereigns could gratify thoſe wiſhes, they were gratified.—Rather, ye buſy Many, learn to pity than condemn the generous frenzy of a bleeding heart which boldly ſacrificed every thing to an over-ruling, an irreſiſtible paſſion—a paſſion mine muſt break to anſwer—and it *will* break.—Oh! my ſhook brain, how wild it wanders!——

* * * * * *

Gay viſions of a higher, happier ſphere, where are ye? ah! deign to gild awhile this gloomy world!—how inexpreſſibly ſweet are at intervals the trances of my mind!——care, ſorrow, ſuffering, mortality itſelf is forgotten; abſorpt in a bright obſcure, every high-wrought feeling hovers on the verge of a long eternity—fye on this earthy

cover-

covering, how it drags down my ſoul, my ſoaring ſoul!

* * * * * *

I wake from theſe day dreams, and return to my ſubject—in fruitleſs and tedious negotiations were thus conſuming thoſe days we would in vain recall, thoſe important days fraught with the very fate of the nobleſt of mankind.

The long delays, the eternal diſappointments, exhauſted my patience; agitated by a thouſand apprehenſions which no leſs concerned my lover than myſelf, miſery once more ſtruck her iron fangs through my quivering heart. Compelled to ſtruggle with a ſoul juſtly conſcious of virtue; to ſupport an apparent tranquillity; to adopt an artificial character, to ſuffer Tiroen to delude himſelf into a perſuaſion that the tye between me and Eſſex was diſhonourable, leſt an uncertain one ſhould want power to reſtrain him, how many implicated indignities did I patiently endure!—Perſecuted with his baſe ſolicitations; overwhelmed with bribes as ſplendid as they were contemptible, I could ward off his expectations only by a feint my nature diſdained. In anſwer to his unbounded offers, and tender proteſtations, I one day bade him remember that in thoſe inſtances he could not ſurpaſs the generous lover he ſought to rival; for that it was in the power of Eſſex to give me every thing but his *title*.—Tiroen pauſed indignantly for a moment, and my heart exulting in its artifice, fondly hoped the ſpectres of his whole line of royal anceſtors would ſweep before him, precluding every idea of a union ſo diſhonorable. His whole eſtimation, and the ſucceſs of the war depended, I well knew, on his retaining the affections of the people, and how could he hope for thoſe if he diſgraced the blood of the O'Neals? He ſcarce credited the boldneſs of idea which appeared in this hint of mine, and ſtruck with a perſuaſion that I muſt be of ſome ſuperior rank to dare thus to elevate my eyes to him, he once more attempted to

dive

dive into a ſecret ſo carefully and obſtinately concealed. I was however on my guard, and ſunk again into my original obſcurity. Still eager to poſſeſs a woman he could not eſteem, he at laſt aſſured me (after having obſerved that an engagement to a lady of his own family alone held his party together) that he would bind himſelf in private by every tye I ſhould dictate. I unwarily replied, the conduct and love of Eſſex had been ſo unqueſtionably noble, that nothing but a ſuperior and public marriage could vindicate me even to myſelf, in breaking with him.—Tiroen's look and anſwer made me ſenſible at once of the danger of this ſpeech, and that in leaving him without hope, I had left myſelf without ſafety. I felt from this moment like a wretch entirely devoted; and under the name of indiſpoſition (of which indeed I had ſufficient reaſon to complain) I procured from a ſurgeon who bled me, a quantity of liquid laudanum, ſome portion of which

I pretended to take every night, but in reality reserved the whole of it for that fatal one which should confirm my fears.

Such were the sufferings of Essex and myself, while the two camps were in sight of each other, and nothing but the most guarded vigilance could prevent the incensed English from coming to action.—I was one evening alone in the tent allotted to me (for Tiroen would never trust me in any neighbouring fort or town), which, from the ascent it was pitched on, commanded the whole valley, and looking with tearful eyes towards the increasing fires in the English camp, when Tiroen approached me unawares—his complexion was flushed with wine, and his eyes and air shewed a determination at which my nature shuddered:—no longer regarding decorum or respect, his manners made me in a moment sensible that I had deferred taking my laudanum too long.—An idea, at which I have never yet ceased to wonder, suggested itself to my mind; and while fluctuating between the possible and im-

impoſſible, I a little ſoothed the boiſterous wretch at whoſe profligate vows I trembled :—intoxication deprived him of the guard he had ſo long kept over his lips —imagining himſelf already poſſeſſed of the beloved of Eſſex, Tiroen could not forbear vaunting of the addreſs which ſecured her to him.—I learnt with equal horror and amazement, that the long delay my capture and the ſubſequent treaties had occaſioned in the war, were all concerted ſtrokes of diabolical policy to ruin the fair fame of the Lord Deputy ;—that during theſe fatal treaties, he himſelf had ſent the moſt indubitable proofs to Elizabeth of the miſconduct of her General, and had every reaſon to ſuppoſe he would immediately be recalled, and ignominiouſly puniſhed—ſatisfied that ſhe could never ſelect another equally dear to the army, on which every thing in war depended.———I turned with ineffable diſdain towards the monſter.——Oh, that an eye-beam could have killed him! —Engroſſed, however, by his various views,

views, inflated with ſelf-love and applauſe, and confuſed with wine, he ſaw not a glance which would inſtantaneouſly have unfolded my whole heart, to the execrable, the ungenerous traitor; unworthy the race he ſprung from, and the ſword he drew.—He continued to expatiate on his hopes of wholly expelling the Engliſh, and aſcending the throne of Ireland: but what after this unwary and black diſcovery could his views be to me? A thouſand dangers were preſſing upon my ſoul, and a thouſand projects floating in my brain: I had hardly temper or recollection to methodize any;—while he continued to charm himſelf with the diſcloſure of all his vanity and ambition, hatred and horror nerved my heart with courage to execute a ſtrange deſign, the deſperation of ſuch a moment alone could have ſuggeſted. Convinced, by the tenor of his diſcourſe and conduct, that I could eſcape his licentious purpoſes only by feigning an intention of yielding to them, I ſmoothed my agonized features into a ſmile which almoſt

moſt ſtiffened to a convulſion, and complained of thirſt—a glaſs of water ſtood by, of which I drank—inclination no leſs than gallantry, made him inſiſt on pledging me; but refuſing to give him the water without wine, I mixed it with an officiouſneſs perhaps but too obvious, adding the whole quantity of laudanum provided for myſelf. The haſte and tremor attending ſo dangerous a tranſaction, might well have excited diſtruſt in him at any time, much more at ſuch a criſis; but not in a condition to obſerve very ſtrictly, and delighted with a condeſcenſion on my part alike new and unexpected, in a tranſport of gallantry he dropt on his knees, and uniting my name with his own, cemented both with that of happineſs: that long loſt bleſſing ſeemed to tremble back into my heart as he eagerly ſwallowed the beverage. Sleep had before hovered over his eyelids; it was now forerun by ſtupefaction. The hour of reſt arrived; but the women who uſually ſlept in the outer tent came not near it—I could not doubt but that their abſence was owing to the previous orders

given

given by the General, and falling on my knees, entreated him who armed the Aſſyrian with courage voluntarily to dare the ſituation into which I was brought unconſenting, to bear me boldly and ſafely through it. A fortitude equal to the danger, ſeemed to ſpring from the addreſs and the occaſion.—The regimental cloak Tiroen had thrown off on entering, ſerved to cover my maſculine habit, which I reſumed with expedition: it was a cloak ſo remarkable, and familiar to every eye in the camp, as almoſt to enſure my ſafety. I overweighed my throbbing temples with his warlike plume, and finally, drawing from his finger a ſignet to produce if neceſſary, I boldly graſped his dagger to decide my fate ſhould I be diſcovered, and iſſued forth a ſecond Judith.

I had warily marked the progreſs of the night; the laſt watch had now gone by, and the time was paſt when it was probable any officer ſhould be ſtirring of note enough to addreſs the General. I had heard Tiroen ſay it was his common practice to walk the camp at night, and

in

in that confidence ventured to paſs for him. Scarce had I gone a hundred paces when the homage of the centinels aſſured me that the counterfeit was undiſcovered.

With an agitated heart I paſſed from one to another, guided only by the diſtant lights (for Tiroen always pitched his camp on a hill) till near the advanced guard; I then retired behind a large tent, and diſrobing myſelf of their General's accoutrements, put on a common hat I had carried for that purpoſe:—what were my terrors when having reached the confines of the camp, now doubly watched, I preſented the ſignet as a proof that I was ſent on earneſt buſineſs.—The guard heſitated, but after tediouſly debating, while I went through tortures, they judged it prudent to admit a token which alone could have enabled me to reach them, and I was ſuffered to paſs.

I ſhot like an arrow from a bow when once theſe dreaded limits were overleaped, ſcarce daring to addreſs my very ſoul to heaven,

heaven, lest one lost moment should undo me.

Whether my eyes had deceived me in the imagined nearness of the English camp, or my trembling and unguided feet had wandered wide of it, I knew not; but sorely were they blistered ere I approached its limits—piercing through thickets which tore alike my garments and my flesh, with spirits fainting even to death, I suddenly heard a scout give the watch-word in English. Overjoyed to think myself safe, I unhappily wanted presence of mind to pronounce a single syllable, and the officious soldier mistaking me for a spy, levelled his piece, and instantly pierced my side—My spirits were no longer equal to contending with danger, or with death, and the fear of discovery being the prevailing sentiment of my sex, I feebly conjured the man, if he hoped for pardon, to bear me to the tent of the Lord Deputy. The delicacy of my complexion and clothes had already surprised the inadvertent soldier—he quickly called together some of his companions, who aſſiſted in laying me on a hurdle, and bearing me toward the tent of Eſſex. The morning was now broke—I ſaw the early beams of the ſun emblazon the golden ornaments of the General's tent—ſome officers came out of it as I approached.—My heart, from which life ſeemed every moment ready to iſſue, made a courageous effort to collect into itſelf the ſcattered principles of a being I appeared on the very point of reſigning. I fancied ere Eſſex yet ſpoke, I heard the voice ſo dear to me—I fancied! ah, I indeed *ſaw* him ruſh forward on the firſt hint; but, root-bound as it were, he ſtopped before he came to me, and ſent his very ſoul forth in a groan.—"Yes, Eſſex," cried I, extending my feeble hand, "the wretch heaven did not allow to live in thy arms, is bleſt with its next indulgence in being permitted to die there."——But how ſhall I deſcribe the tearful tranſports, the touching agonies of his recovered intellects! I ſunk under the keen ecſtaſy of the moment,

ment, and long faintings ſucceeded, occaſioned by my loſs of blood, that once more brought me to the very verge of the grave.

The amiable Lady Southampton came at the inſtance of her couſin, and gave, by her preſence, a decorum to my ſituation it had long wanted. Every effort of art was exerted to ſoothe my broken ſpirits, and ſtrengthen my exhauſted frame. He, who alone could give efficacy to medicine, hovered ever near, and when ſpeech was interdicted, by affectionate looks ſuſtained me.—Ah, how pleaſant were even theſe ſufferings! how delightful was it to collect back into my heart thoſe gentle impulſes war and terror had driven from their home!—to affiance my ſoul in ſilence to its only Lord, and to fancy that whatever fate heaven ſhould hereafter ordain him, mine could no longer be divided from it!

As ſoon as my amended health allowed, I entered into a detail of all that had paſſed ſince Lord Eſſex left me at St. Vincent's

Vincent's Abbey. He in return informed me, that the lethargy into which Tiroen was plunged by the laudanum I had ſo haſtily adminiſtered, was very near being fatal to him, as the utmoſt effort of care and medicine could only preſerve him the faculty of breathing; ſince to diſturb his deep and unwholeſome ſlumbers always threw him into a dangerous delirium. The courageous effort by which I had recovered my liberty, he added, ſtill formed the whole converſation of both camps. I bleſſed the awful power who ſaved me the guilt of murdering even a villain, and did not immediately remark that Eſſex gave me no farther information.

I too ſoon, however, learnt from Lady Southampton the painful truths my Lord ſought to hide—that Elizabeth had inceſſantly urged him to proſecute a war which his fears for me had hitherto ſuſpended; but finding at length that both intreaties and commands were loſt upon him, ſhe at length grew cold and disgusted. His friends in England had given him but too much reason to believe that his enemies were gradually acquiring the ascendancy in her heart, he as gradually lost; since all her favors were lavished on Sir Walter Raleigh, the house of Cecil, and the Earl of Nottingham, a party who had long meditated the downfal of Essex and Southampton, of which they now spoke as a certainty; and that even the common people beheld with discontent the slow progress of the war in Ireland, nor could Essex any longer depend upon popularity.

The unguarded friend who made me this recital, engrossed by her own share in it, forgot how it interested me. I called to mind the information sent by Tiroen to Elizabeth, which but too well accounted for the Queen's anger and disgust, and conceived at once all its probable consequences. Essex, unlike all other favorites, could never be brought to know any claim to superiority but merit——incapable of those little arts

by

by which mean ſouls attach the inſidious train of ſycophants a Court always abounds with; he had ever ſcorned a partial monopoly, and politic diſtribution, of poſts and places.——The mercenary wretches, who had bowed to him in vain, paid their court to his enemies with more ſucceſs, and inſtructed by them in every weakneſs of the favorite, were ever ready to ſtrengthen any prejudice the Queen might conceive againſt him. A thouſand fears incident to age and decaying power were thus cheriſhed in her, which magnified by paſſions time itſelf could never allay, might too probably ſtamp the baſe intelligence of Tiroen with the fatal authority of unbiaſſed truth, and give to the inactivity of Eſſex the appearance of treaſon.—Such a train of circumſtances could hardly fail to ſtagger a mind in full poſſeſſion of the nobleſt and moſt impartial judgment; what then might we not fear from a Sovereign always influenced by prejudices each paſſing day ſtrengthened, by inſenſibly impairing her reaſon? Fortunately, through an extravagance of dotage which almoſt puniſhed the errors of her youth, thoſe prejudices had hitherto united in his favor:—yet while I perceived but a ſingle chance againſt him, my ſoul ſhrunk from the idea of entruſting his life with her.

To give Lord Eſſex the opportunity of vindicating himſelf to Elizabeth, I reſolved to account for her conduct; and divulged to him the inadvertent acknowledgment made by Tiroen, during our laſt memorable interview, of his own perfidy and diſſimulation. A generous ſcarlet burnt on the cheek of Eſſex while he execrated the traitor; but ſtruck immediately with a full conviction of the conſequences that might reſult from this baſe intelligence, he ſuddenly formed the extraordinary reſolution of returning to England to juſtify his honor.

This determination no leſs ſhocked than ſurpriſed me; far from imagining my information would lead to ſo wild a project, I rather ſuppoſed it would ſuggeſt to him the impoſſibility of ever reviſiting England, unleſs the reduction of Ulſter was fully accompliſhed. In truth, I dared

not

not confeſs my fears that even then to remain with the army alone could enſure his ſafety.—Every reaſon I could urge, or Southampton enforce, were however in his judgment feebler than his own—his honor was picqued, and nothing could hinder him from vindicating it.—Perſuaded that a ſtep as bold as this alone would convince Elizabeth of his innocence, and accuſtomed to regain, whenever he appeared, that influence over her, his enemies had often encroached on in his abſence, he aſſured himſelf he need only be ſeen to triumph, and concluded a truce, as the preliminary to his departure.

The pride of ſex, ſenſibility, and honor, contended with the leading paſſion of my nature, and taught me to diſdain over-ruling him I could not convince:—nevertheleſs, I almoſt ſunk under the conflict.—The frightful ſituation in which I had been placed ſince my arrival in Ireland, made me obſtinately refuſe to continue there whenever Eſſex ſhould leave it; and the curioſity I had excited alike by my bold eſcape, and wound, made it hazardous to commit me to the charge of any officer left behind. Surrounded with friends, relations, and dependents, Eſſex (ſuch is the painful uncertainty ever attending on elevated rank) knew not one to whom he could ſafely intruſt ſo delicate a care. The generous Southampton, determined to ſhare the fate of his friend by accompanying him, propoſed to unite that of his Lady with mine, by ſhipping us off ere they embarked, with ſervants they ſhould mutually ſelect; apparently bound for France, but in fact for the coaſt of Cumberland. In the moſt romantic and ſolitary part of that remote county the Wriotheſleys had long owned a caſtle, where malice itſelf would hardly ſeek, and certainly never find us; there he aſſured Eſſex we might repoſe in peace, till they ſhould return again to Ireland. I felt all the merit of this project, by which the amiable Southampton robbed himſelf of the dear ſociety of his wife, merely to do honor to the beloved of his friend; and adopted it with the ut-

moſt

most eagerneſs, from the hope that if the buſy tranſmitters of Lord Eſſex's actions had ever mentioned me, this total ſeparation would extinguiſh all jealouſy in the mind of Elizabeth; who I knew would much ſooner overlook the loſs of an army than his heart.

Although Eſſex knew not how to place me happily in Ireland, it was with pain he conſented to my quitting it; but finding me obſtinately partial to Lord Southampton's deſign, he propoſed my reſuming my maſculine diſguiſe, and ſelected a veſſel whoſe captain was devoted to him, having ordered a lighter one to be prepared for himſelf.

So ſad a preſentiment ſhivered my ſoul on the morn appointed for our embarkation, that it was the utmoſt effort of my principles to ſuffer Eſſex to act in conformity to his. I had previouſly inſiſted that he ſhould ſail at the ſame moment with myſelf, to end my fears of that formidable ſavage Tiroen; and when he entered my chamber to conduct me to the ſhip, my heart quivered on lips which had no longer the power to utter a ſyllable.—He beſought, he conjured me, to ſupport my ſinking ſpirits: "the higheſt hopes," he added, with an air of ſincerity, "elevated his own; that it had always been his pride, his pleaſure, to deſerve the diſtinctions laviſhed on him by the Queen; and whatever views he had formed when heaven ſhould call her hence, he could not reſolve even by ingratitude, much leſs treachery, to ſhorten her days who had crowned his with glory. Doubt not," concluded he, "my love, but I ſhall recover all my influence, and remember when next we meet it is to part no more."

Ill-omened ſeemed that ſentence to me—I fancied too his voice ſounded hollow—I fancied!—alas, every dire chimera ſenſibility preſents to an impaſſioned heart, took full poſſeſſion of mine; yet, as to exert the leaſt influence at ſo trying a moment was to render myſelf accountable for his future fate, I oppoſed every ennobling ſentiment to an ungovernable

paſſion,

paſſion, and heroically reſigned him up to his duty.

We quitted the port at the ſame inſtant; he ſteering for that neareſt the Iriſh coaſt, I for the North of England.—Both by conſent remained on the deck with ſouls fixed on each other, till the beloved individual vaniſhed, and the veſſel ſeemed an object only leſs dear; that at length diminiſhed to a cloud, the cloud ſhrunk to a ſpeck, and the ſpeck became inviſible.—I threw myſelf on my bed, and, giving way to the tears I had hitherto ſtifled, I beſought the Almighty to guard him he had ſo eminently diſtinguiſhed.

Compaſſion had induced Eſſex to conſent to our taking on board an old officer who had been deſperately wounded. The intenſe ſickneſs produced by the element, cauſed his wounds to open, which obliged us to put back and land him, or ſacrifice his life to our convenience; and this unforeſeen delay expoſed us to a calamity as laſting as it was grievous.

Launched

Launched a ſecond time on thoſe reſtleſs ſurges to which alone I could compare my own perturbed ſoul, the next day brought the compariſon ſtill nearer—A dreadful tempeſt aroſe, nor were we within reach of any port. The enraged and howling winds drove the veſſel at pleaſure a thouſand times ſidelong into the deep, and the impetuous and foaming waves threw it up again with equal violence.——We remained ſtupified with terror; ſhut down with our women in the cabin, the rapid motions and cries of the ſeamen, the tremendous cracks and groans of the veſſel, united with the warring elements to make that fate indifferent every moment brought nearer. To prepare my mind for the impending event, I, however recollected, with due gratitude to heaven, that the light veſſel in which Eſſex ſailed, had doubtleſs made a near port, ere the ſtorm began, and landed him in ſafety.

I pondered once more on that wonderful character I had ſo often conſidered. I ſaw, however ſtrong the predominant foible

foible of Lord Eſſex, it ſtill gave way to rectitude; and fearful the paſſion which led him towards me might one day affect his ſafety, I bent to the awful God who thus in thunder called away its weak and helpleſs object; not without admiring the ſingularity of that deſtiny, which by interring me in the ocean, ſecured the forged death and funeral I had publiſhed for myſelf, from ever being diſcovered.

Strengthened, if not conſoled, by theſe ideas, I ſought to cheer my no leſs ſuffering friend; who rejecting alike food and comfort, reſigned herſelf wholly up to ſickneſs, faintings, and ſorrow.—Ah, who ſhall ſay we ſuffer in vain! the feelings of the ſoul, like the organs of ſight, gain ſtrength by uſe, till we dare to analyze that fate we once could not have ventured to conſider; while the refined and exquiſite ſenſe of mental anguiſh, which renders us ſuperior to common evils, often gives an apparent ſublimity to efforts which are little in our own eſtimation.—Lady Southampton, yet diſtinguiſhed by nature, fortune, love, clung to thoſe rich poſſeſ-

ſions,

ſions, and ſhrunk from the awful immortality which threatened every moment to take place of them, while I, accuſtomed to calamity, ſaw in death only its termination.—She liſtened to me with wonder, and this inſtance of fortitude impreſſed her mind with a reverence for my character, time could never obliterate.

The ſudden abatement of the ſtorm contributed little to our ſafety; as the ſhip, ill calculated for ſuch a conflict, had bulged upon a rock, and now filled ſo faſt with water, that the utmoſt diligence of the crew could hardly ſave us from ſinking.—The ſight of land, ere the evening cloſed, had ſcarce power to cheer, for a moment, wretches who no more hoped to behold the dawning of the morn.—To the uproar and turbulence of the ſtorm a ſilent horror and deſolation had now ſucceeded ſcarce leſs ſhocking.—Midnight was hardly turned ere a diſmal univerſal cry informed us that the veſſel was ſinking—Lady Southampton threw her arms helpleſsly round me, and the unprincipled part of the crew, bursting into our cabin, increased the horrors of the moment by opening our coffers, and gathering together their most valuable contents: an officer followed, who taking our hands in silence, led us toward the deck.—two boats were now preparing—the last melancholy hope we had of existence.—The captain, who happily owed every thing to Essex, informed us, that as the larger boat had the better chance, he had fixed on placing us in that, ere the scattered crew could collect, and by pressing too numerously, rob us of a last hope.—We were conveyed into the boat while he was yet speaking, but the sailors so impetuously followed, regardless of the captain's remonstrances and commands, that our danger seemed hardly diminished by the removal.——The change nevertheless encouraged each individual to an exertion from whence the general safety was ascertained. Entirely envelop-ed in the only watch-coat which had been taken from the wreck, Lady Southampton

ton and myſelf (who were the only women ſaved) knew but by the voices of our companions whether life, or death, was to be expected—the ſea ran high, and the grey dawn preſented to our eager eyes a coaſt, which we were informed was that of Scotland, at no great diſtance; an old caſtle appeared, on a ſharp projection of the land, whoſe ſolid battlements ſeemed proof againſt every attack of art and nature; but the ſhoals, rocks, and ſurf that intervened, threatened to make us ever behold it at a hopeleſs diſtance, unleſs we could intereſt the compaſſion of its owners.

Every ſignal of diſtreſs was made for hours apparently in vain, till the turn of the tide; when two fiſhing boats appeared, ſlowly working their way towards us. A diſcordant ſhout of joy on the part of our companions ſplit the ears of my ſick friend and ſelf, who inly worſhipped the power that preſerved us.——The benevolent ſtrangers approached, and their garb no leſs than unknown language

pro-

proclaimed them natives of the Scotch coaſt. To the men around us they offered biſcuits and whiſky in abundance, and beſtowed on me and Lady Southampton a draught of cold water, which ſeemed as much more refreſhing as it was innocent.

Revived by this unexpected revolution in our fate, we by joint conſent ſhook off the heavy watch-coat which had a little ſaved us from the inceſſant ſpray of the enraged ſea, and when the boat was at length drawn towards the flight of rude ſteps leading to the caſtle, we both quitted it with no leſs celerity than thankfulneſs.— Our progreſs was for a moment impeded by ſurpriſe—at the gate of the caſtle ſtood two beings who ſeemed of ſome ſuperior order; ſo ſtrangely was I ſtruck with their dreſs, beauty, and benevolence.— A youth and his ſiſter waved us towards them with graceful courteſy—the latter wore a light veſt and coat of Scots plaid, with a belt of green ſattin claſped with gold; the rude wind had carried off the covering of of her hair and caufed her long auburn locks to ftream on the bofom of the morning, expofing to view her flight ancles half booted, and tinging her cheeks with that pure cold colour, youth, health, innocence, and heaven, alone can give.—The youth, who in features ftrongly refembled his fifter, was habited as a hunter, with a fpear in his hand, and a dagger hanging in his belt.—Both with fmiles of hofpitality ran forward to receive us; and while the young lady took the arm of my friend, the youth with an impaffioned pleafure fhook my hand, cafting a look of mingled wonder and difdain at the foiled, though rich, habiliments I had on; which indeed originally rather agreed with my own fex than that I intruded upon. The antique hall into which they conducted us, was hung with tattered banners, mouldy coats of arms, and every proud remnant of war and ancientry. Refrefhments fuitable to our paft diftrefs were bufily fet before us, nor, with that intuitive politenefs fuperior minds always poffefs, poſſeſs, did either venture to expreſs a curioſity till they had frankly ſatisfied ours.—From them we learnt that the ſpot fortune had thrown us upon, was an iſland on the coaſt of Scotland, and the place which ſheltered us, Dornock Caſtle, held by the Laird of that name; that they were brother and ſiſter to that Laird, who was now abſent on a family concern of no ſmall moment; in ſhort, that their elder ſiſter, Mabel, famed through the country for her beauty, having unhappily ſhewn it at Court, the King would not ſuffer her to return; and their brother, fearful ſhe ſhould yield to his licentious wiſhes, had haſtened thither to claim her. The young people who made this artleſs recital, were formed to grace it— when the fair Phœbe ſpoke of the charms of her ſiſter, her own were heightened by a ſofter, fuller bloom; and when ſhe mentioned their dangerous effect, the proud bluſh of a generous ſhame gave manlineſs to the features of her brother Hugh.——Accuſtomed as my friend and ſelf had long been to every worldly charm and ad-

advantage, we ſaw in this remote ſpot, and theſe untutored children of nature, a ſimple and noble grace art only refines away.

When it came to my turn to narrate, I uſed every artifice to guard againſt the poſſibility of danger.——Adopting the name Lady Southampton had lately quitted, I called myſelf Vernon; a youth employed till lately as a page in the train of the Earl of Eſſex, and now his ſecretary—the lady, with me, I ſaid, allied to the Earl of Southampton, was lately wedded to me; and both were following theſe noblemen when overtaken by the tempeſt which had thrown us upon their ſhore, and rendered us debtors to their humanity. Finding we came from the ſeat of war, and were converſant with the Court of England, they both aſked a thouſand various queſtions ſuitable to their ſex, age, and ſimplicity, reſpecting the one and the other; and our deſcriptions compriſed to them every charm of magnificence, glory, and gaiety.

The

The happy device of a pretended marriage enabling me to ſhare the chamber of Lady Southampton, we choſe the hour of retirement to conſider our preſent ſituation, and the mode moſt likely to reſtore us once more to the country and connections from which the ſtorm had ſeparated us. ——My friend juſtly remarked, that the ſailors wrecked with us, and its natives, were all the people likely to viſit this remote and ſolitary iſle, and that if we failed to take advantage of the departure of the firſt, we ſhould throw ourſelves wholly upon the generoſity of the Laird of Dornock, of whoſe character we could not venture to decide from thoſe of the amiable young people, who had ſo warmly embraced our cauſe.—After the application of Eſſex to my brother in my favour had been rejected, I had every thing to fear if any circumſtance ſhould betray me into his power, and the ſtricteſt ſecrecy on our names and condition alone could give us a hope of liberty;—how under ſuch reſtrictions we could clearly explain our preſent ſituation to the two noblemen whom alone it concerned, neither of us could diſcover; nevertheleſs, neceſſity obliged us to come to ſome reſolution; and perſuaded that the writing of each would be known to him to whom the letter was addreſſed, weary as we both were, a part of the night was ſpent in preparing two epiſtles for the ſailors to convey.—The morning came, and with it the mortifying information that we were a few hours too late; the men ſaved with us having hired a fiſhing ſmack in which they ſailed away at the turn of the tide: nor did its owner know their deſtination till the veſſel returned. I was not without an idea that our youthful protectors had voluntarily concealed ſo material an event in the hope of detaining us; but certainly had that really been the caſe, it was not half ſo inexcuſable as our own imprudence and neglect.—We hired a boat to purſue them with the letters, but after ſeveral days ſpent in painful expectation, the packets were returned to us, with

with the mortifying information that all inquiry had proved fruitless. We had now no resource but in the generosity of the Laird of Dornock, and endeavoured to fortify ourselves with patience to wait his return.

The youthful brother and sister expressed a generous concern for our situation; but wholly without power, they could do no more.—Prisoners at large, as we were, effectually bounded by the roaring ocean, and depending solely on contingencies for freedom, the days to us crept heavily away—I sometimes remembered with a sigh that I was in Scotland—in the kingdom where by inheritance I might claim a rank that would enable me to decide my own fate, had not a combination of events, fore-running even my birth, made every advantage of fortune and nature alike useless to me. I endeavoured to discover the real character of their King, but even from the report of his friends, to be able to term it good, I was obliged to think it weak; and in hat caſe knew he would inevitably be ſurrounded with artful politicians ready to profit by his foible; in ſhort, I found that, however near he and I were allied in blood, we were born to be diſtinct beings in creation, and to meet would endanger the ſafety of the weaker. When I turned my anxious ſoul toward England, it brought me no relief.—As far from the reach of intelligence as if in the wilds of Arabia, I in vain ſought to diſcover the reception Eſſex had met with at Court.—That name, which in the vanity of my heart I often thought the world reſounded with, I found, with checked pride, was ſcarcely known in an adjacent country, till my lips ſo often repeated it; and even when moſt anxious to oblige me, thoſe of others only echoed the ſound ſo dear, ſo beloved! I had but too much reaſon to fear doubts of my ſafety would make him careleſs of his own, and often would have reſigned every brilliant proſpect fancy ever ſpread before me, to aſcertain the life of the Earl.

Too

Too late I regretted the pride of heart which had made me reſiſt the deſire I felt to detain him in Ireland; and could not but acknowledge it was rather that than principle which reconciled me to his departure; yet in a ſituation ſo delicate as ours, to wiſh was to command; and the ſacrifice his own ſoul did not dictate, mine diſdained to ſuggeſt.

My mind now daily paſſed through ſuch a chaos of ideas and emotions, as would have prevented the time from appearing tedious, had not its prolongation been the origin of moſt of them.

Often ſitting on the rude battlements of the caſtle, while the ſurges beat againſt their baſe, have I tuned the lute of Phœbe, and while ſhe warbled a few wild airs of inconceivable melody in a language unknown to me, my full ſoul has wept over the myſterious fate of my ſiſter.—Ah, how eaſy is it to be unknown! —to be entombed alive!—If I, even in a civilized adjacent kingdom, in effect the country of all my anceſtors, can be thus helpless, what may the poor Matilda have been?——Turn, busy imagination, rom the fatal supposition.

The oversight we had committed in suffering the sailors to leave us, became every day more and more regretted.—Lady Southampton soon found herself in a situation that required the tenderest indulgence, and would forbid removal; even if our asylum should be traced by anxious love. We spent our lives in fretting, and had we not possessed an unlimited intimacy, I know not how we should have endured the incessant chagrin.—Deprived even of the usual resources; a scanty library, a lute, some rustic airs, and a pedigree as old as the creation, bounded the possessions and knowledge of our young friends, and could not add any thing to our own.

The Laird of Dornock, however, returned at last.—Ah, how unlike his gentle kindred!—phlegmatic, self-willed, crested, and imperious, his aspect presented a correspondent harshness; and we instantly felt it vain to rest a hope on his friend-

friendſhip: he no doubt reproved his brother and ſiſter for having lived on ſuch familiar terms with ſtrangers, avowedly ſubordinate; and though he often made us ſenſible our company was a burthen, he took not a ſingle ſtep to relieve himſelf from it. Phœbe had begun to improve herſelf in muſic ere his arrival; it was his pleaſure that ſhe ſhould continue to do ſo; but his preſence threw a coldneſs and conſtraint over the whole party, which made what I had once thought a relief, an inconceivable toil. The ingenuous noble girl ſaw her brother's inſolence with a grief which prevented her from profiting by the leſſons ſo much deſired—her guſhing tears would often relax the ſtrings of her lute, while low-warbling tales of hopeleſs love, and her ſad eyes fix themſelves on mine with an expreſſion too ſtrong to be miſunderſtood. I perceived while unconſcious of the danger, becauſe poſſeſſed with the remembrance of my own diſguiſe, that I had won the gentle heart I only ſought to form.—Circumſtanced as I was, this could not but

be

be a dangerous acquifition ; and by a fatality yet more alarming, her elder brother foon after became enamoured of Lady Southampton ; nor did he conceal that inclination—he had from his arrival regarded me with an eye that indicated doubt on the fubject of our marriage ; but the increafing fize of my friend, and our habit of living together, appeared to controvert a fufpicion which neverthelefs remained in his mind.

Anxious to profit by the only hour in the day which could favor his views, he was obliged to give the advantage he fought, and permit me to teach his fifter with no other guard than his younger brother, Hugh, while he paffed the interval with Lady Southampton.—All equally rejoiced at an incident all had equally defired ; as to myfelf, determined from the moment I had been convinced of the paffion of the fair Phœbe, to feize the firft opportunity of intrufting her with my difguife, ere fhame for the miftake fhould difguft her with the object, I was not forry to confide it to

her

her younger brother: as, if it did not more attach him to my intereft, it would at leaft obviate every fear he might entertain on his fifter's account, whom he could then fafely leave at any time. This juft candor produced more confequences than one. The fweet Phœbe ftarted, blufhed, and firft lifting her fwimming eyes toward heaven, fhe then covered them with her hands—when I ceafed to fpeak fhe timoroufly raifed them to my face.—"Ah! why had you not been thus fincere at firft?" cried the generous girl, "the power was then in our hands—*now*"—fhe fhook her head, and in that emphatic gefture ftrongly finifhed her imperfect fpeech. Alarmed and anxious, I conjured her to confide to me thofe reafons which made our fituation in her opinion fo hopelefs. She could not refift my entreaties; and at length acknowledged, "that from the moment her elder brother returned, Hugh no lefs than herfelf had obferved a haughtinefs and feverity in his air and language more forbidding than ufual; at

laft

last they had discovered that their sister, Mabel, far from listening to virtue and the Laird of Dornock, had yielded to the King; and to protect herself from her family, had been compelled to publish her shame, by claiming her royal lover's protection. To reconcile the Laird of Dornock to so cutting a disgrace, a title had been offered him, with any post about the Court he should fix on: and that at length the fair Mabel had consoled herself for the forfeiture of every rational distinction, by the temporary honor of reigning in the heart of her King, and being called a Countess." I inquired with surprise, how an event should affect us in which we apparently had no concern? Hugh answered, "that his brother, far from accepting the splendid coverings offered for infamy, had retired from Court in great indignation; that at first they had both been compelled to scorn and return every letter and present sent by their sister: yet of late some view, inexplicable to them, had made a singular alteration in the Laird of Dornock's sentiments.—

ments.—Several couriers had been dispatched by him to the favorite Countess, but that neither their commissions, nor the answers, ever transpired; yet many circumstances had given them reason to conclude that our pacquets had never been forwarded, as we were taught to believe.—I changed colour at the idea of this deliberate treachery, thanking heaven I alone had been informed of it; as Lady Southampton, often unable to govern her feelings, by some imprudent speech would infallibly have betrayed her knowledge of it. The young Hugh, observing my uneasiness, assured me, "though hopeless of finding a faithful messenger, he held himself answerable for the release of those whom he had contributed to enthrall, and that I might depend upon his own services if I would deign to confide in him, nor should we be suspected as the causes of his disappearance, since the Laird of Dornock well knew his sister Mabel's particular fondness for him, and would naturally imagine that he was determined to profit by the high favor ſhe held at Court."——Is there a charm on earth ſo touching as generoſity?—— The noble youth pauſed with an air that indicated his ardent deſire of having his offer accepted, leſt it ſhould be miſtaken for a vaunt. I took a hand of each young friend, and returning acknowledgments ſuitable to the occaſion, declined embroiling them with their ſullen brother; who could not want power to render our ſituation much more intolerable, if once he ſuſpected us of alienating his family from their duty.—I perſuaded them, as well as myſelf, that our own friends would with unwearied diligence ſearch us out the moment they diſcovered that any part of the crew ſurvived the wreck; of which the Captain would certainly inform them, unleſs he ſunk with the ſhip.

Yet day after day proved this hope vain and fallacious.—A dreary winter paſſed away in this remote Caſtle, through every aperture of which the keen and howling wind poured unreſtrained; and the wild

ocean

ocean ſwelled with frequent ſtorms, while our affrighted ſenſes often miſtook the roar of the tempeſt for the groans of the dying.

I had almoſt ceaſed to hope, when one day, while our hoſt was hunting, I wandered to the battlements as uſual, and deſcried from thence a ſmall veſſel approaching, better built, and more clean, than thoſe I was accuſtomed to ſee; as it drew nearer the land, I perceived Engliſh dreſſes.——My heart took the alarm, I leant impatiently forward, ſtraining the keen ſenſe whoſe imperfection I complained of.—The boat drew near. I diſcerned the regimental of Eſſex; I gave a groan of exquiſite delight, and reeling forward, ſhould have plunged into the ocean, had not the young Hugh, who ſtood behind, held me faſt.—The officer looked up, and I inſtantly perceived him to be Henry Tracey, the favorite aid-de-camp of Lord Eſſex, once before deputed in ſearch of me.—Diſappointment mingled with the various and intereſting emo-

emotions of the moment.—I pointed to the ſtranger, ſighed, and fainted away.

They bore me to Lady Southampton, who thunderſtruck at ſeeing me lifeleſs, and unable to gueſs the cauſe, ſeemed little better herſelf. Hugh, who clearly comprehended from my impaſſioned geſture, how intereſting the arrival of the ſtranger was to me, haſtened to bring him to our apartment, while yet his brother was abſent; when inſtantly retiring, he left us full liberty———"Tracey?" cried both of us at once, "Eſſex?" "Southampton?" echoed each heart, "ſum up all in a word."—"They live," returned he, "and need only behold you to be happy."—"Ah, gracious heaven!" cried I, lifting my eyes thither, while I preſented my heart with my hand to the faithful meſſenger, "receive my tranſport; we now can breathe freely; give us the relief of knowing the events which followed the dangerous voyage of Eſſex and Southampton." "I ſhould hardly dare to do ſo, had I not firſt aſſured you of their ſafety," reſumed Tracey, "for

ſorrow

sorrow I see has been preying already on your bloom; it would not perhaps have been more spared had you passed this trying interval in London."

Apprehensive every moment of an interruption from the Laird of Dornock, we besought the worthy Tracey to dispense with all preface, and hasten his recital.

"With terror and anxiety," continued he, "I followed my Lord into the vessel selected to convey him home, nor were these emotions diminished when I perceived the Lord Deputy full of fits of doubt and reflection, which at times were obvious even to himself; often would he affect to drown them in gay society and wine, and, for the first time in his life, he assumed a false bravery.—At the hours of retirement, far from indulging that intimacy so long established between him and Lord Southampton, of which I had sometimes been a grateful and humble partaker, he sunk into an absence of mind, and total silence, no less alarming to his beloved friend than myself; in effect, that Nobleman saw that he had '*set his for-*

tune on a cast, and he would stand the hazard of the die,' as I conjectured by his turning to me one day, and by an expressive motion of his head, leading mine towards the side of the vessel, where the General leant; his thoughtful countenance apparently fixed on those rolling waves which yet perhaps he saw not.——"All is not well in the heart of thy Lord, Tracey," said his noble friend; then pausing a moment, he added, in a lower tone, "Ah Essex, *aut Cæsar, aut nullus!*" The Lord Deputy happily advanced, and saved me the necessity of corroborating sentiments it gave me pain to adopt.

It was not with the customary greetings we beheld the pleasant shores of our native country—doubt and anxiety had thrown a gloom over those lively and spontaneous emotions, which often suspend even the sense of suffering. Lord Essex lost not a moment, but posted toward the Court, with such expedition, that he outwent all information, and was his own harbinger.—We arrived one morning ere

yet

yet the Queen had left her chamber; but alas, it was no longer the Court we had left—every face around appeared ſtrange to us; and we ſaw too plainly that the invidious Cecils reigned there triumphant. Lord Grey, a favorite of theirs, preſumed to paſs the Earl of Eſſex without notice—that Nobleman gave him only an eye-beam, and haſtened on to decide his fate.—Form was annihilated by circumſtances, and he ruſhed into the preſence of Elizabeth the moment his arrival was announced:—accuſtomed to behold him with complacency, to receive him with kindneſs, the Queen yielded through ſurpriſe to the habits of ſo many years, and granted the private audience he requeſted.—She liſtened to a vague and weak vindication of his conduct in Ireland, and the dotage of her ſoul was perhaps tranſiently gratified with the idea, that he had preferred the recovery of her affection to that of his reputation in arms. After a long conference, the Earl rejoined his friends; pride and pleaſure had flushed his cheek, and the idea of reassuming his accustomed influence, diffused through his mien that benignity and graciousness which are at once its nature and its charm. Resentment and rage never constituted any part of his character, but at the moment he suffered by those passions: such galling sensations were already forgotten.—Overwhelmed with the congratulations of his friends; encircled even by his overawed enemies, the heroic Essex rose above the triumph he could not but desire—every face was instantaneously changed, and those who knew not an hour before whether they should recollect him, now with servile adulation hallowed his very footsteps.—This fatal interval of short-lived power was, however, the last heaven allowed him.—The crafty Cecils and their faction seized the moment he injudiciously quitted the Queen, to persuade her that this indulged favorite had not only acted contrary to his commission in venturing to return himself, but that he had brought home with him all his chosen ad-

adherents, as well as every aſpiring ſpirit likely to ſtrengthen his ſway, and circumſcribe hers.—They touched the ſoul of Elizabeth where it was moſt vulnerable, and having thus oppoſed to each other the two leading weakneſſes of her nature, by throwing the weight of party into the *one ſcale, it ſoon preponderated.* She was unhappily in that declining age which renders every human being in ſome degree capricious and timid.—Already tinctured with fear, ſhe ſoon yielded to the various informations officiouſly brought her by factious confederates.—She was told on all hands that Lord Eſſex was holding a Court even in her Palace, and inſolent and daring as this conduct could not but appear, it was of leſs conſequence than the unbounded influence he ever maintained over the people—an influence he would more than recover the moment he was ſeen in London. "For *themſelves* they heeded not—willing martyrs to their integrity and fealty; but for their Queen, they all trembled at the proſpect."—It was too hazardous to be risqued by Elizabeth; fear and resentment conquered the tender prepossession which still struggled faintly at her heart, and she determined to ascertain her own safety, as well as that of her kingdom, by imprisoning her favorite; nor is this resolution to be wondered at, since even her love conduced to it, when irritated by the imaginary sting of ingratitude. She had set Lord Essex up in early youth as an idol for her own heart to worship; but he was not born to be satisfied with unmerited admiration——the more he acquired the more he sought to deserve; till having established his favor on innate nobleness, he rose above partial distinction, leaving her to lament at leisure the very elevation she had given. From this period she had been weak and irresolute in every instance where he was concerned; at intervals lavishing honors to which he had no title; at others, withholding advantages he had fairly won. The motive of this inconsistency he could not fail to discern, but persuaded an attachtachment which thus powerfully coped with her judgment, was unconquerable, he forgot that ſhe was ſinking faſt into the vale of years, when the nobleſt paſſions inſenſibly condenſe into ſelf-love.

You who ſo well know the heart of my Lord, Madam," cried Tracey, turning to me, "will better imagine than I can deſcribe, his deep ſenſe of an indignity entirely public; and apparently premeditated. So unexpected a manœuvre maſtered his judgment, and giving way to the moſt paſſionate extremes, he drew his ſword, and would have returned it by her meſſenger, beſeeching her "to reward his ſervices by adding a more deciſive blow to that ſhe once before beſtowed on him, ſince both ſeemed to him leſs ſhocking and ignominious than ſuch open and unmerited contumely."——In vain his friends ſought to moderate his wrath; in vain his enemies drew near, eager to catch and treaſure the raſh expreſſions he ſhould unwarily utter, and convert them to his ruin.—Touched on the tendereſt point, his honor, the world combined would have wanted power to ſilence him—he gave full ſcope to his indignant and wounded feelings, and with a ſeverity of truth more galling and dangerous than the greateſt exaggerations, declared aloud, "that the Queen had out-lived all her nobler faculties, and that her ſoul was grown as crooked as her body." This cutting ſarcaſm was too faithfully conveyed to Elizabeth, who regardleſs of his pride while her own was thus wounded, committed him to the charge of the Lord Keeper, whoſe houſe was in effect his priſon.

Oh heavens! what wild viciſſitudes, what tranſports of paſſion took poſſeſſion of my Lord, at recollecting the imprudent readineſs with which he had delivered himſelf helpleſs and unguarded into the hands of his enemies! ſtruggling like a lion in the toils, every vein would ſometimes ſwell almoſt to madneſs, nor dared I leave him a moment alone.

I had no other hope of aſſuaging his irritated paſſions, than by recalling to his mind

mind the beloved image of the fair voyager, to whom the news of this event, and the fear of what might follow it, would, be little leſs than death. I averted one ſtorm however only to give free paſſage to another; the tear of tenderneſs proudly trembled on the burning cheek of anger, and a grief it ſplit my heart to behold, took poſſeſſion of his—"Spare me the killing remembrance," he would cry—"diſgraced—defamed—impriſoned; how ſhall I ever lift my eyes to that fair, that noble ſufferer? I tell thee, Tracey, rather would I have died than known this ſhameful moment."——Impreſſed by the unwearied attachment I had ever ſhewn him, and overweighed by the ſenſe of his own ſituation, my Lord at length condeſcended to lighten his own heart by unfolding to me its deareſt views; well he knew they would never paſs beyond mine—no, every vein of it ſhould crack ere I would wrong ſo generous a confidence, which I acknowledge but to prove my fate wholly dependant on the Nobleman

man I ſerve: I would have it ſo, and heaven could afflict me only by ſeparating them.

The faithful Lord Southampton was his daily viſitant :- though not himſelf a priſoner, the conſciouſneſs that every action of his life was watched and reported, bound that nobleman to a moſt cautious obſervance. The Cecils had now no wiſh ungratified, for the imprudent bitterneſs of Lord Eſſex had ſupplied the only fuel to the Queen's reſentment which could long keep it alive; nor did time, in cooling the paſſions of my Lord, incline him to ſubmiſſion—convinced in his own mind that he was the injured perſon, reflection only ſettled rage into diſguſt and contempt; nevertheleſs, his conſtitution ſuffered ſeverely by this variety of paſſions; when one ſeized upon it, which annihilated all the reſt, and completely undermined his health—a grief more touching than glory or ambition could occaſion ſuddenly ſubdued him.—The time was now come which ought to have brought to him and Lord Southampton the wel-

come

come aſſurance that the partners of their ſouls were ſafe in Cumberland—the time was come I ſay !—alas, it was gone !—Afraid to communicate to each other a terror which preyed alike on both, Lord Southampton diſpatched expreſs upon expreſs in vain.—The days that lingered ſo tediouſly away, however, matured doubt into certainty. Lord Eſſex no longer contended with the nervous fever which obliged him to take to his bed, where reaching out a languid hand to his overpowered friend, he broke, at laſt, the fearful heavy ſilence. "They are gone, for ever gone, my dear Southampton," cried he, in the low accent of incurable deſpair; "heaven has ſpared to ſouls ſo gentle and ſuſceptible thoſe trials our ſtouter minds can perhaps better contend with.—Oh, thou dear one! yet do I regret that this boſom did not receive thy laſt ſighs! that entombed with thee even in the ocean, death had not conſummated a union fortune ever frowned on—but I haſten impatiently to rejoin thee, oh Ellinor! my firſt, my only love!"

The killing remembrance which diſtracted his mind ſoon rendered a malady, ſlight at firſt, deſperate; he was even given over, the Queen for a long time withſtood the accounts given by his friends of his ſituation, ſo deeply had his enemies impreſſed her with the idea that this was only a refined artifice to tempt her to humiliate herſelf. Nevertheleſs, by one of thoſe paſſionate emotions with which nature ſometimes overreaches the moſt elaborate fineſſes of art, ſhe ſuddenly determined to aſcertain his real ſituation, by ſending her own phyſician to viſit him.—The report of that gentleman convinced her of its danger—he was ordered to watch over the Earl with the moſt anxious care; and even to hint to him that every diſtinction would be reſtored with his health.—But, alas! ſympathy itſelf had no longer any charms for him, and the preſence of Lord Southampton ſeemed the only relief his fate admitted. That amiable Nobleman, no leſs ſenſible of the mutual calamity than his

his friend, had not the ſame reaſons to bury his affliction in ſilence.—Repeated meſſengers were ſent alike to Cumberland, and the port you embarked from, ladies: thoſe who returned from the latter only confirmed the fears which had hitherto fluctuated—they informed the lover and the huſband, that the wife of the Captain mourned for him as dead, nor was it doubted but that the crew and paſſengers were alike victims to a ſtorm ſo ſudden and tremendous. The active and enlivened ſoul frequently exhauſts its moſt acute ſenſations by anticipation.—Certainty could not add to the grief occaſioned by ſurmiſe; and the extinguiſhed hopes of the friends gave them alike up to that cold and ſullen deſpair, which is the worſt of all ſtates, becauſe frequently incurable. Thoſe late hopes the Queen was willing to revive her dying favorite with, made not the leaſt impreſſion on him; and the Cecils learnt with ſurpriſe, that, neither their views, their conduct, nor even his own diſgraceful

ful imprifonment, any longer touched Lord Effex; nay, that not even his recovery was able to revive thofe habits of enterprize the world were taught to think hitherto uncontroulable. His friends, on the contrary, bleft the fkilful phyfician who prolonged a life fo valuable, and faw with the happieft hopes, that thofe romantic flights in his character his enemies had almoft wrought up to his ruin, were at once extinguifhed; leaving it without any other diftinction than a melancholy fweetnefs which rather turned his thoughts toward philofophy than war. The people, ever naturally difpofed to fide with the unfortunate, cried out, that he was the innocent victim of the Cecil party; who by fome odious ftrokes of policy, added popularity to their depreffed rival, in diminifhing their own——Elizabeth herfelf could no longer fupport the idea that the man fhe ftill loved was obfcurely breaking his heart, while yet in the flower of youth, in an unmerited and difgraceful prifon.—She yielded to the information of the

the physician that my Lord's amending health required air, and sent him her permission to retire to any of his seats in the country; but forbad him to attempt appearing in her presence: a restriction perhaps more agreeable to Lord Essex, than herself, could she have seen the desolate situation of mind in which he departed.

From the country he addressed a letter of thanks to the Queen, which displayed at once his eloquence, gratitude, and languor: in truth, the latter gained ground daily in his character. Lord Essex was born capable of uniting in his person every various and generous pursuit, had fortune allowed it, but not even he was equal to living without one.—I frequently trembled at beholding his gloom and inanity. Wholly withdrawn from the sphere in which he had hitherto moved, and the pleasures he had once enjoyed, the rude society of his neighbours, and the boisterous amusements the country afforded, rather offended, than employed an enlightened and susceptible heart. He wandered

dered all day in the woods alone, and returned every evening ſpent and unrefreſhed, only to recover animal ſtrength enough to enable him to paſs the morrow in the ſame melancholy manner.

In this ſituation I fancied a falſe hope could not add to his danger, and might perhaps rouſe thoſe active faculties every hour ſeemed more and more to abſorb. I one day ventured to repeat to him an imaginary dream, tending to prove that you ſtill exiſted.—Not even the firmeſt mind can reſiſt the ſubtle attacks of ſuperſtition when labouring under depreſſion.—His ſoul ſo eagerly adopted the fiction of my brain, that I was a thouſand times tempted to acknowledge it to be ſuch, but dared not venture to ſhew him I had played upon his wounded feelings. Revived with the moſt vague and diſtant hope, he impatiently drove me away on a ſearch my own ſoul foreboded to be fruitleſs. I even debated after I ſet out, whether I ſhould not loiter out the appointed time in England till I could decently return from

my

my imaginary peregrination, when a dream, more pointed and singular than that I had feigned, awakened in myself those hopes I had communicated to my Lord, and led me from isle to isle enquiring for you: but I will not call it a dream, since surely the event proves it a visitation.—Oh, gracious God! what joy will my return pour into the hearts that now ach for either! How pure will be the satisfaction derived from their acknowledgments!"

During this long recital, my tumultuous feelings pursued my love through every desperate situation.——My woe-struck heart hardly dared to breathe, till finding him at last free and well, it gave a deep sigh, and respired without pain. Essex insulted, endangered, imprisoned:——I cast my eyes round those gloomy walls, I so late thought my prison, and raising them to heaven, adored the power who there confined me, unconscious of the conflicts I could not have supported. Ah, Essex! what were the warring elements, the midnight wreck, the long, long ſolitude, the dire uncertainty I had ſo bitterly bewailed, to the ſingle idea of ſeeing thee one moment at the mercy of Elizabeth, one moment in the power of thy enemies! And yet, for me thy generous ſoul loſt all ſenſe of even theſe inflictions; pride, vanity, and grandeur, in vain aſſailed thee: a true and noble paſſion beat unalterably at thy heart, condenſing in one favorite ſorrow, thoſe mighty powers, which once fulfilled every various and active duty of humanity.

But this was not a time for impaſſioned reveries. Lady Southampton recalled my attention to the preſent moment; and we employed it in informing Tracey of the name, character, and ſituation, we had thought it prudent to aſſume, as well as thoſe of our hoſt. Scarce was he maſter of theſe important particulars, ere the Laird of Dornock returned, and broke in upon us with an abruptneſs and anger he took no pains to diſguiſe. The ſight of an Engliſh officer

officer a little abated his wrath. Tracey, according to the plan we had agreed on, called Lady Southampton his ſiſter, and, with every teſtimony of gratitude for the hoſpitable ſhelter our hoſt had ſo long given us, offered a recompenſe ſtill more agreeable; with which happily he had had the forecaſt to provide himſelf.—While the Scot ſtood irreſolute reſpecting his anſwer, the wary Tracey turned to us, and, in an authoritative voice, ſaid, he muſt anſwer to the Queen for his abſence, did it exceed the appointed time; and therefore, we muſt quickly take leave of our friends, and haſten our departure for England. This deciſive ſpeech increaſed the perturbation and diſappointment already obvious in the features of our hoſt; nevertheleſs, our going was to him ſo unforeſeen an event, that, not being able to find a ſufficient reaſon for detaining us, he tacitly conſented to it.

My heart bounded at the unhoped-for liberation, and I would have failed that moment, deſpite of wind and tide; but, as the ſailors declared this impoſſible, our departure was delayed till the next morning. Whether the various incidents of the day accelerated the hour appointed by nature, or that Lady Southampton, contrary to her own idea, had reached it, I know not; but ſhe was ſeized at midnight, with the pains of labour, and ſuffered ſo ſeverely, that her life was depaired of. In the courſe of the enſuing day ſhe was delivered of a dead child, and I was obliged to conſole myſelf for the long delay this event muſt neceſſarily occaſion, by the pleaſing idea that the partner of my fate was not prematurely divided from it—in truth her vexation was ſo great, that I was reduced to ſtifle my own, leſt I ſhould contribute to her illneſs.

The fate which hope yet gilds, though but from the verge of the horizon, is never quite inſupportable. We found, in the protection of Tracey, and the idea of rejoining the world, to which he ſeemed our immediate link, the means of beguiling many a tedious hour; nor was

this

this consolation superfluous; for the Laird of Dornock became, from the moment of Tracey's arrival, more sullen and impenetrable than ever.—Self was, in him, the prevailing principle. Early invested with that bounded, but absolute, authority, which oftener produces and shelters tyranny, than a more extensive field of action, he had hitherto known no opposition.—How often has a blind passion warped the noblest natures! nor was it perhaps unnatural that he should stretch his prerogative, to retain in his hands a lovely and beloved woman, over whom he could claim no right.—Long inured to fear, suspicion, and anguish, they readily returned to their throbbing habitation, my heart. I often fancied I read murder written in dark, but legible lines, on the knit brow of our host; and though Tracey slept only in an outer chamber close by us, scarce could I persuade myself that he was suffered to rest peaceably there, or yet lived for our protection: nevertheless, I strove at times to reject those black chimeras a lively imagination perhaps too readily adopted.

The Laird of Dornock no longer interfered with us, or our fate; neither did he withhold from us the company of his fister.—That fweet girl, new to fociety, with a romantic happinefs peculiar to youth, gifted every object with her own graces and virtues: impreffed at once with the merit of Tracey, fhe transferred to a heart which could deferve it the paffion I had unwarily infpired, nor was her fecond choice unpropitious. Tracey, whofe foul had expanded in a camp, was yet to learn the inconceivable charm of love: it took full poffeffion of him. With a fweet, though fad pleafure, I witneffed pure and innocent vows, which continually reminded me of thofe days, when like Phœbe, I looked enraptured on the varied landfcape of life, yet glowing with the early beams of hope; unconfcious of the fhowers which often would fall, the heavy nights which muft wholly obfcure it. Tracey, no lefs delighted than his miftrefs, no longer haftened his departure to England, and looked

aftoaſtoniſhed that we did not find every charm of exiſtence in this diſmal exile.

I, however, anxiouſly waited, with Lady Southampton, for the day when her recovered health ſhould enable us to depart.—It came at length, and we were eagerly preparing for the voyage, when the Laird of Dornock ſent us an order to read, by which the King of Scots impowered him to detain us. I know not any ſhock, of all fate had impoſed on me, I ever felt more ſenſibly: nevertheleſs, I had preſence of mind enough to obſerve, by the date of this order, that it had been obtained during the confinement of my friend. The diſappointment and deſpair this incident occaſioned, was only alleviated by the recollection that in abuſing the authority of the King, to indulge an unworthy inclination, the Laird of Dornock had made himſelf reſponſible to the laws of his country for our ſafety, by admitting that ſuch perſons were in his cuſtody. Tracey gave him notice of this immediately; and though he moderated his rage in consideration of the fair Phœbe, he warned the Laird of Dornock to treat us nobly, as he would answer it to his own King, and the Queen of England, in whose name we should soon be demanded. To this indignant vaunt, for in truth it was no better, the haughty Scot coldly answered, "that he should take his chance of incurring an old woman's anger, who perhaps had already resigned all her rights to his master." Tracey could no longer controul the feelings of his generous soul, and replied with acrimony. The Laird of Dornock bade him profit by the occasion, and be gone immediately, if he did not mean to be included among the prisoners. There wanted only this stroke to consummate our wretchedness, and, however reluctantly we resigned our only friend and protector, Lady Southampton joined me in urging him to go: till, over-ruling all his objections, we hastened him alone into a bark, which an hour before we seemed to see ourselves in. He comforted us with

with the aſſurance of ſoon returning, being fully perſuaded the King of Scots would never authorize ſo unjuſt and illegal a procedure, when once the whole circumſtance was impartially ſtated to him. I ſighed, at remembering I knew him better; but as an explanation at that moment was vain, I urged not the unbounded influence of the fair Mabel, through whoſe illicit connection with the King this order had doubtleſs been obtained. How indeed ſhould that Monarch be convinced of a remote act of injuſtice, who even at the moment of committing it, was wronging every moral and religious duty? The man who once voluntarily errs, muſt either be weak or vicious; in the firſt inſtance, he reſigns himſelf up to the paſſions of others, in the latter to his own; and in either caſe ſcarce ever recovers the narrow but even boundary of virtue.

It was not by ſuch means I hoped for freedom—ah, no! my views all pointed toward the lover to whom my heart like the

needle

needle ever vibrated, though far divided. —Let Essex be once informed, sighed I—let him once know where to find me, and he would cross the globe to ensure my safety. When the chagrin of this trying moment abated, I called to mind the infinite relief the visit of Tracey had given our spirits, and the change it had made in our situation, by acquitting us of those petty obligations which always humiliate a noble mind, unless it finds a congenial one in the bestower.

I soon observed that the Laird of Dornock had not courage to profit by the base injustice he had committed. The subservient situation Tracey had placed himself in, whenever we were present, and the profound deference with which he obeyed our every wish, neither agreeing with the rank we avowed, nor the regimental he wore, a vague idea of mystery had taken possession of our host's mind, which wanted vigor and activity to attempt developing it. Conscious too late, that he had, in releasing Tracey, set a spy on his own

conduct,

conduct, he vainly regretted the timidity which prevented his detaining him. He nevertheless, at intervals, still talked of love to Lady Southampton, offering to buy a return by imaginary worlds of wealth: for to us, accustomed to elegance and luxury, all his possessions appeared but a gaudy poverty. As these ostentatious and absurd offers were one day made in my presence, I could not but take some notice of them; he silenced me however, by replying, that I must be cautious how I exerted a spirit so likely to make him transfer his attachment, and be satisfied with protecting one of the two; since I could neither think so ill of his discernment, or my own beauty, as to believe him the dupe of my disguise. As it was the first time a doubt on the subject had ever transpired, my confusion gave him a full conviction: I could not recover myself sufficiently to reply for some moments. at length I told him that he had guessed the only part of our secret which did not lie too deep for his knowledge;

ledge; neverthelefs, that all he had difcovered, was but the leaft part of the myftery; and finally that the day which informed him of our names and rank, would call him to a fevere account, if his conduct were in the leaft unworthy either of us or himfelf.—I boldly added, that the only thing ever wanting to our fafety, was, to have the Court of England informed of our afylum, and now that was by Tracey's means afcertained, we were not without noble friends to claim us. The grandeur of air natural to me when infult roufed my pride, aftonifhed and awed the Laird of Dornock; his mind laboured with vague and indiftinct apprehenfions; and as all attempts at diving into a fecret locked up folely in the hearts interefted in retaining it, muft be vain, he half repented having exerted an unjuftifiable influence, he could no longer hope to profit by.

Lady Southampton acknowledged her obligations to my firmer fpirit; and both having no farther reafon to affect fubordination, refumed the habits of rank and

and diſtinction; hiring domeſtics of our own till the moment of enfranchiſement ſhould arrive.

Heartily weary of us both, I often thought the Laird of Dornock meditated propoſing to releaſe us, and while I was one day inſenſibly guiding him to that wiſhed-for point, an order from Court was delivered into his hand. Convinced that it would liberate us, I caſt an eye of triumph on him, while he opened it; and ſaw his countenance confeſs the ſame idea; but a moment cauſed a viſible change in it. He read the order aloud, and we found with inexpreſſible aſtoniſhment, that it contained the ſtricteſt charge to guard his Engliſh priſoners, as he would anſwer it to his King: yet with all due deference.—I eagerly caught at this article, without ſeeming to notice the firſt, which nevertheleſs ſunk deep into my heart; nor was his inſenſible to the latter.—The wearineſs and diſguſt he had begun to indulge, increaſed; and his pride revolting at the idea that his caſtle was become a ſtate priſon, and himſelf only a jailor, he felt every way irritated, humiliated, and offended. No human being submits to power with so ill a grace as the man who has unjustifiably exerted it, and when its restrictions fall heavily on such, mere retribution becomes in effect a severe revenge.

A tedious interval had again elapsed without any news from England. The tender, timid Phœbe often persuaded herself that her lover had never reached it; and the singularity of finding ourselves apparently forgotten, sometimes inclined my friend and self to unite with her in that opinion—yet, how many other causes might we reasonably assign for the neglect —causes, so much more afflicting, that we recalled our thoughts to the isle for consolation.

Whether the infinite variety, the eternal transitions my own life had already afforded, inclined me to hope on; or, whether the incessant prayers I addressed to him who alone could relieve me, endued my mind with fortitude, I cannot say; but, I certainly daily discovered in it re-

sources

ſources hitherto unknown. Every paſſing hour ſeemed to refine and ſettle its powers and perceptions, till thoſe turbulent paſſions, which of late ruſhed like a cataract through my frame, now, with a gentle, healthful current, gave motion to my pulſes.

We learnt from Phœbe, that many letters came from Mabel to her elder brother, the contents of which he ſo cautiouſly concealed, as made it obvious we were their ſubject. This news only confirmed us in the belief that Tracey had reached England ſafely; and afforded us at the ſame time the flattering idea, that our friends were anxiouſly labouring to recover us; however their progreſs might be impeded by obſtacles, we could neither gueſs at, nor decide upon: nor were theſe ſuppoſitions vain. An order at length arrived that we ſhould be delivered to the officer who ſhould preſent its counter-part. Oh, what joy, what gratitude, what anxiety, did this proſpect of a deliverance afford us! From the dawn of the morning till night blackened the ocean, did one or the other

watch

watch with eager expectation the promised vessel.—We beheld it at last, and hardly could Essex himself have been more welcome to my eyes.

Tracey once more landed, and glad was the greeting on all sides.—He presented each of us letters—dear and precious characters! my soul poured through my eyes when I again beheld them! With lavish tenderness Essex hailed my second resurrection, and vowed to shew his sense of the blessing by an implicit submission to my will.—"You shall no more complain of the terrors of a camp, my love," continued he; "I turn for ever from the bloody scene.—A court no longer has any charms for me: inspired with juster sentiments, alive to purer pleasures, in your heart and my own will I henceforth look for the wayward straggler, happiness. I am no longer, my sweet Ellinor, the Essex you have known! I am become an absolute rustic, a mere philosopher. With you I will abjure the world, and in some solitary spot, devote myself to love and the sciences. Oh! shut

ſhut your heart, like me, my love, to the paſt, and look only towards the future. I wait with impatience the news of your ſafe arrival in Cumberland, and date from that day our happineſs."

Theſe words were to my ſoul, what the balmy breath of ſpring is to the frozen earth: the winds at once ceaſe to blow, the ſnow ſinks into her boſom, the buds put forth their verdure, and nature forgets ſhe has ſuffered.

Tracey came fraught with gifts rather ſuited to the ſpirit of the donor, than that of the accepter; yet, they opened the heart of the Laird of Dornock, who liſtened to the avowal of Tracey's love without repugnance; and at length promiſed him his ſiſter, if, at the expiration of two years, his rank in the army entitled him to claim her.—The tears of the young lovers for ever cemented thoſe vows his will thus authorized. Joy having diſpoſed my heart to receive the ſoft impreſſions of every gentle paſſion, extinguiſhing all that were not ſo, I remembered, with astonishment, the moment when I readily adopted the ambitious projects of Essex.—Rank, riches, glory, what are ye?—Gay ornaments which lend splendor indeed to felicity, but which only incumber and weigh down the soul when struggling with the waves of misfortune: gladly we lighten ourselves of such adventitious goods, and grasp in tranquillity and love, the unenvied, but rich essence of all our fortune.

In life, as in prospects, we can long enjoy only a bounded view; and all which present, either to the mind or eye, a multiplicity of objects, however great or beautiful, overstrain the faculties, and destroy the pleasure. Rejecting at once every gaude vanity delights in, from the distant throne, and the mighty multitude, ready perhaps in turn to conduct me to it, my soul called forth the beloved individual, and seating him at my side in a safe and humble solitude, asked what we should lose by the change?—lose! Ah! rather what might we not gain?—How

sweet

ſweet was it then to find that Lord Eſſex himſelf at length cheriſhed ideas wholly ſimilar; that, weary of war, ambition, envy, and all the turbulence of life, in renouncing the court of Elizabeth, he left, with the power, the wiſh of poſſeſſing it!—That time, ſolitude, reflection, diſappointment itſelf, had rather refined than extinguiſhed his taſte, which thus regained its true bias · ſeeking in the powers of the mind, and the impulſes of the heart, a happineſs not to be found on earth, when thoſe ſources fail to ſupply it.

In leaving for ever the dreary ſcene of my exile, I could be ſenſible of only one regret: but flattering myſelf, that Tracey would ere long reſtore the ſweet Phœbe to my friendſhip, I ſoon dried up the tears due to the floods that charming girl beſtowed upon our parting. The rapid motion of the veſſel bore no proportion to my impatience; whenever I looked, that deteſted iſle was ſtill in view; I thought we ſhould never loſe ſight of it.

Oh! how I anticipated the ſweet repoſe which awaited us in the green ſolitudes of Cumberland! I flattered myſelf that Eſſex would already be there; though Tracey aſſured me, ſpies ſtill followed his ſteps, from which only a long confirmation of his peaceful intentions could relieve him.

At length the pleaſant ſhore of England was deſcried; welcome to my heart was the ſhout which proclaimed it! Our very ſouls ſhot through our eyes once more, to hail our native country. We found at the port, ſervants, and every accommodation that might render our journey eaſy. Ah! how beautiful was that journey!—a thouſand various objects of ſimple majeſty united to form one perfect whole; and a new delight ſtole on every ſenſe, as we wound through varying vallies embowered by hanging woods, which were reflected in many an expanſe of water, and dim ſhadowed at intervals by mountains whoſe arid heights defied the ſun they ſeemed to ſwell to.

Far

Far in these green labyrinths we came at once upon the Castle from whence I now write.—It is in fact only an elegant ruin, and might rather be termed the residence of the anchorite, Solitude. In tearful gladness the fair owner threw her arms round my neck, and blest the power which permitted us at last to rest here.

From this antique mansion do I date my narrative; and, in arranging it, seek only to fill up those hours yet unblest with the presence of him born to fill every future one. Dear Lady Pembroke, I cannot express to you the divine repose which hushes at last my overworn faculties. —I look back with wonder on all the past griefs, the mortal conflicts, my shattered frame has contended with. So pure, so perfect, is now my grateful tranquillity, that it seems proof even against misfortune itself.—No more shall my beating heart—my burning brain—but why should I revert to such dismal recollections?

Embosomed in the maternal arms of nature; safe in the obscure and solitary ſituation of this ivied aſylum, here my affrighted ſoul, like a ſcared bird, faintly folds up its weary wings ! delights to be alone, and joys in mere ſafety. I think I can never be happy, be grateful enough, and while my heart exhauſts itſelf in enjoyment, I ſtill call on it for ebullitions to which it is unequal. Pride, paſſion, vanity, all the groſſer particles of my nature are at once exhaled, and every pure, every ſocial virtue, unfolds and bloſſoms to the vernal ſun, forerunning even the ſnow-drop.

Oh ! that radiant, glorious luminary ! how new to me ſeems its influence !—Dark have been the films through which I have hitherto viewed it. Pardon, my darling friend, theſe flights of fancy : how playful does the mind grow when at peace with itſelf !

Haſten, generous Tracey, haſten to my love, and inform him of our arrival. But is not Tracey already gone ? Oh ! haſten then, my Eſſex ; quit that buſy ſcene, where virtue inceſſantly hovers on the verge of a precipice a thouſand ready

ready hands would plunge her over,—partake with me the deep repose of this solitude—no longer heed Elizabeth herself; not even her power can reach us here. Nature's gigantick phalanx, impassable mountains present their formidable summits in long array, overawing every inferior guard, while, in their vivid hollows, happiness reposes on the bosom of her mother, Nature.—Oh! come then, and in

> "*A life exempt from public haunt,*
> "*Find tongues in trees, books in the running streams,*
> "*Sermons in stones, and good in every thing.*"

* * * * * * *

A thunder-bolt falls on my brain! Avenging heaven, why does it not wholly split it? Tried—sentenced—condemned—while I, entombed in a now detested solitude, gaily dreamt of endless happiness.—Oh! let me once more rush madly into the world, overwhelm my agonized ſenſes with the ſhouts of armies—the groans of the dying—fountains of blood—rivers of tears—find if poſſible a horror in nature may counteract that now raging in my ſoul.—The wreck of the univerſe alone can equal it.—But let me give the ruin ſcope—wherefore, wherefore, ſhould I wiſh it leſſened—Oh! Lady Pembroke!

LADY PEMBROKE WRITES.

The trembling hand of the friend laſt invoked, takes up the pen to finiſh the woes of a fair unfortunate, who will never more be her own hiſtorian.—Alas, they had now reached their climax.

The eccentric turn of mind which made the ſweet Ellinor form a plan ſo extraordinary as her ſuppoſed death and burial, excited an aſtoniſhment in me, its artful execution alone could increaſe. Nevertheleſs, the regular purſuit of a ſingle idea was far from perſuading her friends, that her intellects had recovered their tone, or equality.

When

When this heart-breaking narrative came to my hands, I could not but observe that the ſweet miſtreſs of Eſſex had a very partial knowledge of his character, or information of his actions.—Bleſt with the moſt equitable and generous heart that ever actuated a human boſom, that nobleman's virtues often took a falſe color from the ſelfiſh views of thoſe who once found the way to it. Credulity was ſo much his fault, that even his enemies profited by it, whom he always ceaſed to conſider as ſuch, the moment they deigned to deceive him with a falſe proteſtation of regard—In fact, the lenity of his nature continually counteracted that ambition, which was its only vice; and irradiated his character with the milder glories of humanity; a luſtre, more ſoft, pure, and laſting, than mere conqueſt can beſtow. Nevertheleſs, the early habits of power and diſtinction had ſeized on his affections, and even his love co-operating with that indulged foible, they increaſed together. The daring project he had formed was

no

no way unfeasible, had he managed it with address: for he possessed the hearts of the whole kingdom, a few envious individuals excepted. But art was unknown to Essex; and those his superiority offended, were proficients in that science: unhappily too, they were so immediately around the Queen, that they could convert the suspicions she sometimes entertained of his conduct, into certainty. Yet so rooted was her love for this unfortunate favorite, that it long contended with that she bore herself; and tears of ill-judged fondness have often absorbed the bitterness his enemies would have wrought to his ruin. Such a weakness alone could induce a sovereign, wise and experienced like Elizabeth, to delegate a power scarce inferior to her own, into the hands of a Nobleman, valiant, popular, and aspiring. In consenting to Essex's command in Ireland, the Queen made an absolute sacrifice of her own inclination (which was only gratified when he was near her) to his; or, perhaps, in effect,

both

both unconsciously yielded to the secret policy which invariably sought to separate them.—Convinced she had bound him to her by every tie of gratitude, honor, and confidence, how must so high a spirit as that of Elizabeth be shocked, wounded, and irritated, to see her favorite loiter away his days inactively in Ireland, regardless alike of her admonitions, and the censures of the people!—Insensibly she imbibed the prejudices of the Cecil family, the inflexible enemies of the Earl; to whom she submitted the government of the state, less from any esteem for their talents, than the latent desire of piquing the negligent Essex, to whom they were equally obnoxious. Time confirmed to the Cecil faction, the influence they at first owed solely to resentment. The wearisome supineness of the Lord Deputy was at once succeeded by a suspicious, and mysterious conduct. His secret treaties with the arch-rebel, Tiroen, the anonymous captive who seduced him into these—all was reported with ag-

gravation

gravation to Elizabeth. The resentment occasioned by the error of his conduct, was doubled when she knew that of his heart: jealousy took full possession of hers, and she determined to make him severely sensible of her power; but she was told it was not safe, at that period, to recall him. Obliged for the first time in her life to controul herself, and meditate how to get him again into her power, her temper became absolutely intolerable. Her Ladies preserved a melancholy silence, save the artful few won over to foment, and profit by, her irritated passions. The fate of Essex seemed wholly to depend on the event of a war, hitherto unprosperous; when to the astonishment alike of friends and enemies, without performing any considerable exploit which might secure him a welcome, the Earl posted suddenly home, and presented himself before Elizabeth, with the dauntless air of unblemished innocence. Whether the surprise of the moment really revived that powerful passion of which

he

she had so long been the object, or whether fear for her life made her dissemble the bitterness and rage swelling at her heart, is a circumstance which never reached my knowledge. It is certain the Queen received him graciously, and listened to a very imperfect and incoherent defence of his conduct. They parted friends; and Essex instantly giving way to that credulity, which so often made every talent art and nature could unite in his person abortive, considered himself as effectually re-established in her heart, and indulged all the exultation such a triumph over his enemies could not fail to occasion.

What a thunder-stroke then was his immediate disgrace! a disgrace he could not but impute to his own imprudence; since in returning without advice, he had delivered himself voluntarily into the hands of his enemies. To the mortification of a long and humiliating imprisonment was shortly after super-added a killing grief, in the supposed loss of the beauteous Ellinor.

Re-

Resigning himself to a sullen and silent despair, Essex no longer condescended to offer Elizabeth any further vindication of his conduct, nor could be persuaded to make the least submission. This concussion of feelings, however, shivered his animal, no less than his mental, system. A fever followed, which soon rose to a dangerous height. Obstinately rejecting all medical advice, he declared a thousand times that he wished only to die: nor had the wish been vain, but that the Queen, unable wholly to subdue the sentiments of tenderness which had so long reigned in her heart, sent her own physician to attend him, with offers of peace and pardon. The desperate state in which he found the Earl, was faithfully reported to Elizabeth; who, touched to the heart, hesitated whether she should not revive him by an immediate visit; so hard will it always be to counteract by political manœuvres the genuine impressions of nature. The Cecil party suddenly found themselves on the brink of ruin; and every argument, fear, pride, or prudence, could ſuggeſt, was enforced to delay this interview. Elizabeth yielded to the powerful combination of reaſons in that inſtance, but could not deny herſelf the pleaſure of correſponding with Lord Eſſex as he grew better; and ſoon ſuffered him to vindicate his conduct: nay, even condeſcended to reproach him with the unknown lady who had ſo fatally influenced it. To this perplexing hint, he replied, his grief alone muſt anſwer; and the melancholy tenor of his life ſo exactly agreed with this declaration, that Elizabeth preſſed no farther into a ſecret it was plain the grave now veiled: rather ſeeking by kindneſs to invigorate a mind ill-fortune had borne too hard upon.

It was now the ſhining time in the life of Eſſex. The purple torrent of ſucceſsful war had hitherto ſwept away, or ſunk, thoſe ſweet humanities, thoſe ſocial virtues, time at length brought to light in the vale of adverſity.—Endued with eloquence,

quence, taſte, ſcience, ſenſe, and ſenſibility, he now reſigned himſelf to the charms of philoſophy, poeſy, and the mathematicks: innocent and tranquil reſources, to which the mind muſt ever turn when diſappointed, if bleſt with powers capable of reliſhing them. The Cecils never thought Eſſex more dangerous. Age and infirmity now made Elizabeth anxious for peace abroad, and tranquillity at home, and there wanted only a meeting between her, and the altered Earl, to re-eſtabliſh him in her favor: but that meeting his enemies entered into a league to prevent; and began, by winning Elizabeth's phyſician to order the Earl of Eſſex into the country.—An artifice ſo refined as his liberation was not immediately diſcovered to be policy by any party; and the Queen lulled into a belief that ſhe could honorably receive him when he ſhould return, ſuffered him to depart without an audience.

Wearied of wars, camps, and political jealouſies, and diſcuſſions, the melancholy Eſſex deſired in freedom only the ſolitude he found; when Tracey returned with the aſtoniſhing news that the miſtreſs he ſtill adored yet exiſted. —Fatal news to his future repoſe!—The impoſſibility of openly claiming Ellinor, revived with his paſſion all his dangerous and precarious projects.—Every other effort to obtain her was made without ſucceſs, ere he ſecretly applied to the King of Scots, who always knew his own intereſt too well to grant any favor without having ſecured an adequate return. James ardently deſired to be nominated as the ſucceſſor of Elizabeth by herſelf, and had not ſpared bribes, promiſes, or flattery, to intereſt thoſe around her whom he thought likely to influence her choice. The unhoped overtures of the man whoſe courage and ambition James moſt feared, was a circumſtance of importance. Uninformed of the real name or characters of the priſoners Lord Eſſex ſo eagerly deſired to recover, the King of Scots ſent the Laird of Dornock notice to guard them more ſtrictly. The impetuous temper of Eſſex made him always reſign to the prevailing object, every other intereſt: but a treaty like this could not be carried on ſo ſecretly as to eſcape the ſuſpicious eyes of the miniſters. With what malignant joy did they ſilently watch its progreſs till the moment when its publication would inflame the Queen to their wiſhes!

Eſſex now once more thought it his intereſt to be buſy, admired, and popular: he relapſed into all his old habits, and, having won the Queen's permiſſion, returned to London. Far, however, from profiting by this indulgence, to re-inſtate himſelf in her favor, he remained entirely at home; throwing open his doors to all impoveriſhed officers, and clergy, among whom a number of ſpirited adventurers appeared, whoſe laviſh praiſes ſeemed to render his popularity greater than ever.

Elizabeth, with diſguſt, beheld him aſſume the diſtinctions ſhe perhaps intended once more to beſtow; and kept in ſilence a ſtrict watch upon his conduct. By a re-

refinement, known only in politicks, his enemies ſcattered among his partizans many creatures of their own, inſtructed to dive into all his intentions, and ſpread abroad ſeditious and treaſonable projects, as though intruſted by himſelf with ſuch. This malice was but too ſucceſsful.— Inflated with the adulation of misjudging friends, the extravagant admiration of the multitude, and the inſidious attacks of his enemies, the deluded Eſſex ſprung the mine himſelf by which he was deſtroyed.

The miſchief commenced by a broil between the Lords Southampton and Grey; the laſt aſſaulting the former in the ſtreet; and, though the offender was ceremoniouſly puniſhed, the ſpirit of party broke out in a thouſand little daily quarrels. The Queen, already perſuaded that Eſſex, ever haughty and impetuous, ſcorned her power, deſpiſed her perſon, and only waited a favorable moment openly to inſult both, was irritated beyond all endurance by the artful discovery (at this cruel crisis) of his secret treaty with the King of Scots. Its real cause was unknown to her, and the offence, though trifling in itself, of a nature most likely to exasperate a Sovereign whose eyes were ever turned from a successor she refused to acknowledge.——The discovery proved decisive—Elizabeth instantly resolved to deliver her ungrateful favorite up to the laws of his country, and authorized a judicial inquiry into his conduct. The Cecil party desired no more; for well they knew, Essex would rather die than brook the deliberate indignity. The commissioned Lords assembled at his house on a Sunday, as the time when they should be most safe from the insults of the partial populace.—They found the Earl sufficiently inflamed, who, swearing he never more would become a voluntary prisoner, shut up the Lord Keeper, and the rest, in his own house, rushing forth armed, and followed only by a few friends and

do-

domeſtics to claim the protection of the people.

By a fatality not peculiar to himſelf, the bubble, popularity, which had ſo long ſwelled and glittered before his miſtaken eyes, burſt at once, and left to him a vacuum in nature. The ſacred day was but too judiciouſly choſen by his enemies.——Without preparation——almoſt without a friend, the unhappy Eſſex ruſhed through the ſtreets of London, crowded only with peaceful and humble mechanics, who emerged from every cloſe lane environed by their wives and children to enjoy the weekly holiday.—To people of this ſtamp the gallant Eſſex was almoſt unknown—certainly indifferent; with ſtupid and curious eyes, they turned to gaze on thoſe warlike ſteps none ventured to follow—ſteps which bore the noble Eſſex ſo faſt toward ruin. Diſtreſs, however, only increaſed his deſperation, and the citizens being ſpirited into making an ineffectual effort to prevent his return, a ſkirmiſh enſued. The amiable Tracey had the fate he deſired, and fell at the ſide of his Lord; who, even in this cruel moment, dropt a tear on a youth ſo beloved. Fame, honor, happineſs, nay, even life, were fleeting faſt from Eſſex; and however careleſs of theſe goods, friendſhip ſtill aſſerted her rights over his feelings—In compaſſion to the few generous adherents who muſt have fallen in his cauſe, had he longer reſiſted, the Earl at length ſurrendered his ſword.

All was now over with this admired, and erring favorite.—Impriſoned in the Tower he had ample leiſure to re-conſider the events which brought him there.—The deſertion of the people had opened his eyes to the realities of life.—He too ſenſibly found, that, while he miniſtered to their neceſſities, their pride, or their pleaſures, the multitude could rend the air with acclamations; but that the moment a claim is in turn made on their feelings, they always become cold, torpid, and inanimate. He perceived with vain

vain regret that he had been duped into this outrage on the laws of ſociety, by the manœuvres of his enemies, no leſs than the credulity of his heart. But Lord Eſſex was not formed to profit by theſe humiliating diſcoveries; they impreſſed a nature ſo generous, only with the deepeſt diſguſt.—He was, however, conſoled with remembering that ſelf-preſervation was the ſole motive for his daring attack, and that no action of his life had yet violated the duty he had ſworn the Queen. He reſolutely prepared himſelf to meet the judgment of his peers, and only lamented the friendſhip which involved the generous Southampton in his fate; who ſhared without regret the priſon of a friend ſo dear.

The Queen, meanwhile, experienced every emotion ſuch a painful contrariety of paſſions muſt neceſſarily occaſion.—The impriſonment of her favorite, as uſual, ſeemed to cancel his offence: but he was now beyond her juriſdiction, and the victim of the laws. She had un-

 happily

happily ſurrendered him up to them, and robbed herſelf of every prerogative but that of pardoning; a prerogative ſhe feared ſo high a ſpirit would never ſolicit her to exert.—She regretted, too late, having driven him to ſo dangerous an extreme, and while his fate was yet uncertain, ſuffered more, perhaps, than he did in its completion.

The friends of the Earl, perſuaded that no kind of influence would be ſpared to bring him to the block, were unanimous in intreating him to win over the Queen by an early repentance and ſubmiſſion: but they knew not the grandeur of the heart they would have humbled.—Born to diſtinguiſh himſelf moſt eminently when outward diſtinctions were withdrawn, it was then only Eſſex ſeemed to uſe his better judgment. "Can any one call himſelf my friend," would he indignantly exclaim, "and yet wiſh me poorly to petition for an obſcure, an ignominious life? What! to pine away the flower of manhood in infamy and ſolitude! ſhunned by all yet unſtigmatized by public juſtice,

and

and ſhunning, in turn, the exalted characters I dare no longer emulate.—Shut up with thoſe tormenting companions, my own thoughts, till led, perhaps, by deſperation, to inflict that fate upon myſelf, I have meanly evaded receiving from the law.—No, my friends, I am enthralled here as a traitor—if proved one, it is fit I expiate my crime; and if acquitted I know the value of a life ventured hitherto only for my country."——Neither arguments, or intreaties, could ſhake his reſolution; and he heard with unequalled firmneſs that public ſentence, from which, he ſtill perſiſted, there was no appeal. In vain every dear and affecting image was pourtrayed in the ſtrongeſt colours before his active imagination.—From that of the woe-ſtruck Ellinor, liberated too late, and weaving in a diſtant ſolitude a thouſand fairy bowers for love and happineſs to dwell in—from her alone his nature ſhrunk. "You may wound my heart," would he ſighing ſay, "through every vein; but my reaſon is ſtill inflexible, nor is even that ſweet

creature

creature an argument for my ſubmitting to diſgrace.—No! when I raiſed my eyes to thee, dear Ellinor, my conſcious ſoul beheld in itſelf all that could intitle me to mate with thee.—I cannot reſolve to look up even to the woman I adore.—Better ſhe ſhould weep me dead, than ſecretly deſpiſe me while yet exiſting.—Pure and precious will be the tears that fall upon my grave, but never could I behold one which would not ſecretly reproach me.———Leave me, my friends, to my fate; honor has hitherto been the invariable rule of my conduct, nor can I now adopt another."

From the moment the condemnation of Eſſex reached the Queen, peace and reſt were ſtrangers to her.—The choſen of her heart was now the victim of the laws, and that heart muſt bleed through his, unleſs he could be induced to throw himſelf on her mercy. A thouſand emiſſaries aſſured him of a ready pardon——a word, a wiſh, would have obtained it.—To theſe he ever replied with the ſame collected

lected air, "that had the Queen earlier shewn him this indulgence, his life had never come within the censure of the law; but as even her utmost bounty now could only prolong to him the liberty of breathing, he was willing, as well for her safety as in submission to his sentence, to resign a privilege, which had been a burthen the moment it became his only one." An answer thus calculated to touch the most indifferent heart, stabbed that of Elizabeth: yet as, unasked, to grant him a pardon, would stamp her declining life with inexcusable weakness, she underwent every hour the most trying conflicts.

Ah! why do I say the most trying? alas, there was a fair, and forlorn one, buried in Cumberland, who more than died when this cruel intelligence reached her. As the sentence of Essex extended to his friend Southampton, the relations of the latter dispatched an express to his wife, hoping she would arrive in London time enough to solicit his pardon of the Queen.

Queen. The meſſenger found the unfortunate Ladies buoyed up with ſafety, ſolitude, and many a gentle hope. When the approach of horſes echoed through the remote valley, no other emotion was excited in either, than the fond and latent flutter ariſing from the idea that it might be one or both of the condemned Earls.—How terrible was then the tranſition in their minds, when fully informed of their deſperate ſituation; and bereft of every reſource expected miſery ſupplies! The unhappy wife of Southampton, engroſſed by her own ſhare in the affliction, obſerved not its deep, its deadly effect, on the intellects of her equally ſuffering friend; till the ſtupefaction of Ellinor became intenſe, and obvious, and the evil irremediable.

The human mind, even when moſt elevated, is not equal to the influence of two oppoſing paſſions—a ſacrifice muſt be made, and friendſhip yields to love. Lady Southampton poſted away with unremitting diligence, intruſting her

friend

ſriend to the care of faithful ſervants, who were directed to bring her forward more leiſurely.—The deep gloom of the ſweet Ellinor's mind, in the courſe of the journey, gave way to a vague and irregular gaiety; but as this had ſometimes forerun her recovery, ſo might it then, had ſhe been ſurrounded with ſuch perſons as knew her diſpoſition.—Thoſe who had her in charge, uninformed of her name, ſituation, and wounded ſpirit, could not reaſonably be expected to guard againſt events they could not poſſibly foreſee. It happened, one day, that while they were reſting, Ellinor caſt her eyes upon an extenſive building, full in ſight, and her wandering imagination called it Kenilworth.—An officious attendant informed her it was Fotheringay Caſtle.—She wildly ſhrieked, ſtretched forth her arms expreſſively towards the fatal manſion, then tearing thoſe lovely treſſes once before devoted to her calamity, and ſcarce grown to their uſual luxuriance, threw herſelf on the ground, and relapſed into total inſanity.

But

But when Lady Southampton entered the prifon of her Lord, upon whofe aching bofom fhe poured forth all her grief and paffion, his difturbed friend found every fibre of his heart wrung; and turning a fearful, eager eye toward the door, felt a horror not to be expreffed, at finding no one followed her.—The afflicted wife wanted prefence of mind to conceal a truth which confummated the fate of Effex—a truth fo terrible, that fain would he have believed it invented by his friends to reconcile him to his fentence.—Convinced at length—"now indeed do I feel the weight of my bonds—now indeed am I a prifoner," would he exclaim.—"Oh, Ellinor, matchlefs Ellinor, that I could fly to thee! recall once more that unequalled foul, which always, like a frightened bird, forfakes its home when mifery hovers over it.—Thou, thou, haft broken a fpirit equal to every other affliction—thou haft made a coward of me—to fave thee, my love, I could almoft refolve, poorly to condition for a difgraceful life, and wifh to furvive my honor."

Per-

Persuaded that his presence would have the same effect it once before took at St. Vincent's Abbey, he passionately solicited to see her.——This single idea seized upon his mind—it even became his solemn request—his dying wish.—In the hopeless state of her disorder the effect of their meeting was dreaded only on his account; but as intreaty and argument proved vain, his friends at length resolved to yield to his passionate, his only solicitation. The day was now appointed for the execution of Essex, and the pardon of Southampton granted, which alone he desired;—as all his friends were freely admitted to his person, there was no difficulty in leading thither the darling of his heart, in the habit of a youth, accompanied by Lady Southampton.——Worlds could not have bribed *me* to witness such an interview.—Ah, dearest Ellinor! were those senses they so eagerly desired to restore to thee, in reality a loss? How, had they been perfect, wouldest thou have supported the trying scene, expiring love, and officious friendſhip, dragged thee to witneſs ?—How wouldeſt thou have fixed thine eyes on the gloomy tower, or thoſe guarded gates through which thy lover muſt ſo ſoon be borne, but never more ſhould paſs ?—How muſt thy ſoul have bled to behold thoſe fine features a few hours were to ſeparate from the heart which then gave them ſuch agonized expreſſion ! But that ſuperlative miſery was not ordained thee.—Retired, beyond the reach of love itſelf, were all the various powers of that ſuſceptible ſoul !—Thy vague eyes confeſſed not their everlaſting object—thy ear caught not his voice—nor did thy boſom anſwer with a ſingle ſigh, the burſts of grief which ſtruggled at that of thy lover, ſtill exquiſitely alive to every human affliction ! To thee his parting ſoul yet clung ; and when his eyes beheld thee no longer, they willingly ſhut out creation. He ſaw not, from the moment of Ellinor's departure, friend or relation ; but turning all his contemplations towards

the

the awful futurity in which he was so soon to launch, died to this world even before his execution.

On the night which preceded that event, this billet, equally addressed to my sister (with whom the dear unfortunate resided) and myself, was delivered.

"Dear, generous guardians of the lost angel my soul yet bleeds over, receive in this my parting blessing; and pardon, oh, pardon, an incredulity but too severely punished by conviction! a conviction so terrible as reconciles me to the death to-morrow will bestow. Yes, these eyes have been blasted with beholding the pale statue of my love, dead while yet breathing—speechless—insensate.——-To the gathered multitude—the fatal scaffold—the axe which separates soul and body, I turn for relief when this remembrance presses upon me.

"Adieu, ye faithful sisters of the gallant Sydney—Oh! if intelligence too late should visit the fair form bequeathed to your friendship, with sympathy soothe every aching sense.———Yet 'wake no more to woe my worſhipped Ellinor !—Still may thy pure ſpirit ſlumber in its breathing tomb, till that appointed hour which at length unites thee to thy

ESSEX."

Tower.

It ſeemed as if in this epiſtle he enclosed every lingering weakneſs of mortality; for the remaining hours of his life were devoted ſolely to the duties of religion.—In the flower of manhood, at the age of three and thirty, this envied favorite reſigned every earthly diſtinction, and aſcended the ſcaffold with a compoſure innocence and Heaven alone can beſtow. The melting multitude too late bewailed to ſee his glorious youth ſet thus in blood.—His ear caught the general murmur of ſorrow and applauſe; he caſt a look of corrected knowledge on the ſpectators; then lifting his eyes to Heaven, ſerenely ſubmitted to the executioner; who ſevered a head and heart, which, had they acted in uniſon, might have awed the world.

Of

Of her ſo much beloved, ſo generouſly, ſo fatally faithful, little more remains to be ſaid.—Neither time, care, or medicine, ever availed toward the reſtoration of thoſe intellects which might only have proved an additional misfortune—Yet even in this ſtate of inſanity, Heaven permitted her to become the inſtrument of a ſingular and exemplary vengeance.

A year or more had elapſed, during which her calamity took all thoſe variable and dreadful forms peculiar to itſelf.—The deſire of having every medical aſſiſtance made me often bring her to London; where one evening, with a degree of reflection and art ſometimes blended with inſanity, ſhe eluded the care of her attendants; and well knowing every avenue of the palace, paſſed them all with wonderful facility.

The Queen wholly ſunk in the chilling melancholy of incurable deſpair, and hopeleſs age, reſigned herſelf up to the influence of thoſe evils.——Her ladies were frequently employed in reading to her, which was the only relief her chagrin admitted.——One memorable night it was my turn—Elizabeth dismissed every other attendant, in the vain hope of finding a repose of which she had for ever deprived herself. I pursued my task a long while, when the time conspired with the orders of the Queen to produce a silence so profound, that had not her starts now and then recalled my senses, hardly could my half-closed eyes have discerned the pages over which they wandered.—The door flew suddenly open—a form so fair—so fragile—so calamitous appeared there, that hardly durst my beating heart call it Ellinor. The Queen started up with a feeble quickness, but had only power to falter out a convulsive ejaculation. I instantly remembered that Elizabeth believed her dead, and imagined this her spectre. The beauteous phantom (for surely never mortal looked so like an inhabitant of another world) sunk on one knee, and while her long garments of black flowed gracefully over the floor, she lifted up her eyes toward Heaven, with that nameless sweetness, that wild ineffable benignity, madness

neſs alone can give; then meekly bowed before Elizabeth.—The Queen, heart-ſtruck, fell back into her ſeat, without voice to pronounce a ſyllable.—Ellinor aroſe, and approached ſtill nearer; ſtanding a few moments, choaked and ſilent. "I once was proud, was paſſionate, indignant," ſaid the ſweet unfortunate at laſt, in the low and broken voice of inexpreſſible anguiſh, "but Heaven forbids me now to be ſo—Oh! you who was ſurely born only to chaſtiſe my unhappy race, forgive me—I have no longer any ſenſe but that of ſorrow."——Again ſhe ſunk upon the floor, and gave way to ſobbings ſhe ſtruggled in vain to ſuppreſs. The Queen dragged me convulſively to her, and burying her face in my boſom exclaimed indiſtinctly,—"ſave me—ſave me—oh, Pembroke, ſave me from this ghaſtly ſpectre!"—"Eſſex—Eſſex—Eſſex!" groaned forth the proſtrate Ellinor, expreſſively raiſing her white hand at each touching repetition. The violent ſhudderings of the Queen, marked the deep effect that fatal name took on her.—"Somebody told me, continued the lovely wanderer, that he was in the Tower, but I have looked there for him till I am weary—is there a colder, safer prison, then? But is a prison a place for your *favorite*, and can you condemn him to the grave?—Ah gracious Heaven, strike off his head—his beauteous head!—Seal up those sparkling eyes for ever.—Oh, no, I thought not," said she with an altered voice.—"So you hid him *here* after all, only to torment me.—But Essex will not see me suffer—will you, my Lord? So—so—so"—the slow progress of her eyes round the room, shewed, she in imagination followed his steps.—"Yes—yes,"—added she, with revived spirits, "I thought that voice would prevail, for who could ever resist it?—and only I need die then; well, I do not mind that—I will steal into his prison and suffer in his place, but be sure you don't tell him so, for he loves *me*—ah! dearly does he love me, but I alone need sigh at that, you know."

And

And sigh she did indeed.—Oh! what a world of woe was drawn up in a single breath!—The long silence which followed, induced the Queen once more to raise her head—the same sad object met her eyes, with this difference, that the sweet creature now stood up again, and putting one white hand to her forehead, she half raised the other, as earnestly demanding still to be heard, though her vague eyes shewed her purpose had escaped her.—"Oh, now I remember it," resumed she, "I do not mind how you have me murdered, but let me be buried in Fotheringay; and be sure I have *women* to attend me *be sure* of that—you know the reason." This incoherent reference to the unprecedented fate of her royal mother, affected Elizabeth deeply.—"But could not you let me once more see him before I die? resumed the dear wanderer.—Oh! what pleasure would it give me to view him on the Throne!—Oh, I *do* see him there!" exclaimed she in the voice of surprise and transport. "Benign, majestic!—

Ah, how glorious in his beauty!—Who would not die for thee, my Effex!"——"Alas, never, never, never, fhall *I* fee him!" groaned forth the agonized Elizabeth.——"Me married to him!" refumed our friend, replying to fome imaginary fpeech,—"oh, no, I took warning by my fifter!—I will have no more bloody marriages: you fee I have no ring," wildly difplaying her hands, "except a black one; a *black* one indeed, if you knew all—but I need not tell *you* that—have I, my Lord?—look up—here is my love—he himfelf fhall tell you." She caught the hand terror had caufed Elizabeth to extend, but faintly fhrieking, drew back her own, and furveyed it with inexpreffible horror. "Oh, you have dipt mine in blood!" exclaimed fhe, "a mother's blood! I am all contaminated—it runs cold to my very heart.—Ah, no,—it is—it is the blood of Effex; and have you murdered him at laft, in fpite of your dotage, and your promifes? murdered the moft noble of mankind! and all becaufe he could

could not love you. Fye on your wrinkles!—can one love age and uglineſs?—Oh, how thoſe artificial locks, and all your paintings ſickened him!—How have we laughed at ſuch prepoſterous folly!—But I have done with laughing now—we will talk of graves, and ſhrouds, and church-yards——Methinks I fain would know where my poor ſiſter lies buried—you will ſay in my heart perhaps—it has indeed entombed all I love; yet there muſt be ſome little unknown corner in this world, one might call her grave, if one could but tell where to find it: there ſhe reſts at laſt with her Leiceſter—he was your *favorite* too—a bloody, bloody, diſtinction."——The Queen, who had with difficulty preſerved her ſenſes till this cutting period, now ſunk back in a deep ſwoon.

The diſtreſs of my ſituation cannot be expreſſed.—Fearful leſt any attempt to ſummon a ſingle being ſhould irritate the injured Ellinor to execute any dire revenge; for which I knew not how ſhe was prepared, had not Elizabeth at this juncture loſt her ſenſes, I really think mine would have failed me. I recollected that the Queen by every teſtimony was convinced that the unhappy object thus fearfully brought before her, died in the country long ſince; nor was it wiſe or ſafe, for thoſe who had impoſed on her, now to acknowledge the deception. "So—ſo—ſo," cried Ellinor, with a ſtart, "would one have thought it poſſible to break that hard heart after all? and yet I have done it—She is gone to—no, not gone to Eſſex."———"Let us retire, my ſweet Ellen," ſaid I, eager to get her out of the room, leſt the Queen ſhould ſuffer for want of aſſiſtance.—"Huſh," cried ſhe, with increaſing wildneſs, "they will ſay we have beheaded her alſo.—But who are you?" fixing her hollow eyes wiſtfully on me, "I have ſeen you ſomewhere ere now, but I forget all faces in gazing on his pale one.—I know not where I am, nor where you would have me go," added ſhe, ſoftly ſighing, "but you look like an angel of light, and may be, you will carry me with you to Heaven." I seized the blessed minute of compliance, and drawing her mourning hood over her face, led her to the little court, where my servants waited my dismission; when committing her to their charge, I returned to wake the ladies in the antichamber, through whose inadvertent slumbers alone, Ellinor had been enabled to pass to the closet of the Queen; a circumstance which combined with a variety of others to give this strange visitation the appearance of being supernatural.

Every common remedy was tried in vain to recover Elizabeth, and the applications of the faculty alone could recall her senses; but the terror she had endured shook them for ever. Shuddering with apprehensions for which only I can account, she often holds incomprehensible conferences; complains of an ideal visitor; commands every door to be shut; yet still fancies she sees her, and orders her to be kept out in vain. The supposed disregard of those in waiting incenses a temper so many causes concur

to

to render peeviſh, and her unmerited anger produces the very diſregard ſhe complains of. Rage and fear unite thus to haraſs her feeble age, and accelerate the decay of nature. When theſe acute ſenſations ſubſide, grief and deſpair take poſſeſſion of her whole ſoul;—nor does ſhe ſuffer leſs from the ſenſe of her decaying power. Unwilling to reſign a good ſhe is unable to enjoy, ſhe thinks every hand that approaches, is eager to ſnatch a ſceptre, ſhe will not even in dying bequeath. Oh, ſweet Matilda! if yet indeed thou ſurviveſt to witneſs this divine vengeance, thy gentle tears would embalm even thy moſt mortal enemy! thou couldeſt not without pity behold the imperial Elizabeth, loſt to the common comforts of light, air, nouriſhment, and pleaſure; that mighty mind which will be the object of future, as it has been of paſt, wonder, preſenting now but a breathing memento of the frailty of humanity.—Ah, that around her were aſſembled all thoſe aſpiring ſouls whoſe wiſhes centre in dominion;

minion; were they once to behold this diſtinguiſhed victim of ungoverned paſſion, able to rule every being but herſelf, how would they feel the potent example! Ah, that to them were added the many who ſcorning ſocial love, confine to ſelf the bleſſed affections which alone can ſweeten the tears we all are born to ſhed!—Gathering round the weary couch where the emaciated Queen withers in royal ſolitude, they might at once learn urbanity, and correct in time errors, which, when indulged, but too ſeverely puniſh themſelves.

* * * * * *

Abſorbed and blended in the buſy and woful ſcenes this heart-breaking hiſtory preſented to my mind—an anxious partaker in each ſucceeding calamity—I ſeemed to live over again the melancholy years we had been ſeparated, in the perſon of my ſiſter.—My own misfortunes—my darling daughter, the whole world vaniſhed from before my eyes—deep-fixed

on

on objects no longer existing, or existing but to double my affliction: I remained almost the statue of despair; every sense seeming rivetted on the manuscript I held; and buried in so profound a reverie, that Lady Arundell judged it prudent to interrupt it. The consolatory reflections her friendship dictated, died on my ear, but reached not a heart which deeply pursued the sad chain of ideas thus presented to it.—Starting as from a frightful sleep, I, at last, sunk on my knees, and raising my eyes, with the manuscript, at once toward Heaven—"Oh, mighty Author of universal being!" sighed I, "thou who hast lent me fortitude to struggle with almost unequalled trials, support my exhausted soul against this last—this greatest.—Let not the killing idea that it is a *human* infliction, trouble the pure springs of piety, whence alone the weary spirit can draw consolation.——Rather strengthen me with the holy belief that it is thy visitation for some wise end ordained; so shall my enemies sleep in their

graves

graves uncursed, and my heart remain in this agitated bosom unbroken. Alas, who knows but by thy divine appointment, I may be at last permitted to recall the scattered senses of this dear unfortunate? to soothe that deeply-wounded, that embittered spirit! Ah, Ellen!—Ah, my sister!" groaned I, deluged at last with salutary tears,—" changed—lost—annihilated as thou art, my unaltered affection must ever desire thee.—I need not inquire whether she is here—your sympathizing, generous tears, dear Lady Arundell, inform me that the same roof shelters the twin heirs of misfortune."

Although Lady Arundell acknowledged that my sister was under her protection, fain would she have persuaded me to delay a meeting so touching, till more able to support it; but, deaf to the voice of reason, nature, powerful nature asserted her rights, and my soul obeyed her impassioned impulse. The deep, the eternal impression of this agonizing meeting, recurs even now with all its first force. I had ſhuddered at the murder of my mother—I had groaned on the coffin of my huſband—I had wept a thouſand times over the helpleſs infant who trembled with my boſom—but all theſe terrible ſenſations were combined when my ſad eyes reſted on thoſe ſtill ſo dear to me—when I ſaw all their playful luſtre quenched, and ſet in inſenſibility—when I felt that heart, once the ſeat of every feminine grace and virtue, throb wild and unconſcious againſt one which I thought every moment would eſcape from its narrow boundary.—But let me quit a ſcene too trying for recollection—too touching for deſcription. Oh, Ellinor—my ſiſter!

THE

RECESS, &c.

PART VI.

TIME, which inures us to every kind of ſuffering, at length ſtrengthened my mind againſt the heavy ſadneſs impreſſed on it by the fate of this dear unconſcious ſufferer. It was with true gratitude and concern I learnt that Heaven had called to itſelf the amiable and accompliſhed ſiſter of Lady Arundell, who caught a cold during her attendance on the ſick Queen, which ended in a conſumption, and carried her off a few months after Elizabeth. Actuated to the laſt by the ſublimeſt ſympathy and friendſhip, Lady Pembroke had added, to the moiety of the ſurveyor's treaſure (which ſhe had cauſed to be dug for in the ſpot ſpecified) a ſufficient ſum to ſecure the dear unfortunate Ellinor every comfort her forlorn ſtate admitted; placing with her Althea, the favorite maid ſhe had ſo tenderly commemorated, and committing both to the charge of Lady Arundell; who with equal generoſity received ſo anxious a truſt. A virtue thus conſummate ſanctifies itſelf, and can receive neither glory or grace from the gratitude of humanity; yet ſurely the incenſe of the heart ariſes even to heaven! accept it then, oh, gentleſt of the Sydneys, although inſphered there!

The ſtrange and unaccountable difference in my ſiſter's opinion and my own, reſpecting Lord Leiceſter, ſupplied me a ſource of endleſs meditation. yet, as this difference became obvious only from the

the time we arrived in London, I could not help imputing her blindneſs to the ſame cauſe ſhe aſſigned for mine.—Certainly ſhe imbibed the unreaſonable prejudices of Lord Eſſex; whoſe ambition (however fatally expiated) always inclined him to diſlike a Nobleman born every way to ſuperſede him. I ſaw but too plainly from the irritation and vehemence to which her temper from that period became ſubject, how much a woman inſenſibly adopts of the diſpoſition of him to whom ſhe gives her heart. I had not however looked on her choice with the contemptuous aſperity with which ſhe regarded mine.—Lord Eſſex, I will frankly own, ere yet he roſe into favor, was gifted like my ſiſter with every captivating advantage of nature.——The fire and ingenuouſneſs which afterwards marked his character, then lived only in his eyes: and the cultivated underſtanding he poſſeſſed, pointed every glance with elegance and expreſſion. One muſt have loved Lord Leiceſter to ſee Eſſex with indifference—one muſt have loved him to the exceſs

I did perhaps, not to remark the attachment my ſiſter now avowed.—Innumerable inſtances of it flaſhed on my memory which I was aſtoniſhed could at the moment eſcape me. If *ſhe* was indeed more clear ſighted than myſelf—But why do I enter on ſo vain a diſcuſſion?—Alas, dear Ellinor! beloved Leiceſter! I have no right but to lament ye.

I had likewiſe gathered another painful doubt from the ſtory of my ſiſter. England had gained a King in the ſon of Mary Stuart, but her unfortunate daughters muſt not hope to acquire a brother. From the moment I had been informed that mine had acceded to the throne, the tender mother's heart hàd fluttered with the idea of preſenting to him the lovely girl ſo nearly allied to his blood. Although regardleſs of diſtinction in my own perſon, I could not turn my eyes on the fair daughter of Lord Leiceſter without coveting for her every human advantage.——Unwilling to be ſwayed by prejudice, I ſeparately conſulted with the

few

few friends fortune had left me; who all concurred in giving me an impreſſion of the King, degrading, if not contemptible. They repreſented him as national, vain, pedantic, credulous, and partial: wanting generoſity to beſtow a royal funeral on the body of the royal martyr, his unhappy mother; yet daily impoveriſhed to meanneſs by favorites and paraſites. Enſlaved by the imperious ſpirit of a Queen he neither loved nor valued; and only endeared to the people he governed through the fickleneſs of their natures, which are always gratified by change. As thoſe who ſpoke thus could have no poſſible intereſt in vilifying or depreciating him, I could not but give ſome credit to their account; and made it my firſt concern to ſee the King; anxious to read in his countenance a confutation of every charge. How unaccountably was I diſappointed when my ſenſes took part with his enemies!—I beheld with aſtoniſhment, in the perſon of James, youth without freſhneſs, royalty without grandeur, height without majeſty——an air of ſlyneſs and a ſecret ſervility characterized features, which, though devoid of the graces of either diſtinguiſhed parent, wanted not regularity; and a ſtooping ſlouch gait gave an invincible awkwardneſs to a figure nature had endued with ſymmetry. Offended and repelled, my heart ſunk again into its own little manſion, nor claimed the leaſt alliance with his.—I determined to watch at leiſure his real character and conduct, nor ventured to confide to his care the ſingle treaſure Heaven had permitted me to retain, of all it once beſtowed. Reſolved to educate my daughter ſuitably to the rank ſhe ought to have held, I thought it wiſe to bury in my own boſom, at leaſt for a time, the ſecret of her right to it; and the eccentrick turn of mind every ſucceeding day rendered more obvious in the King, made me continually applaud the moderation and foreſight which had guarded me on this intereſting occaſion.

I, how-

I, however, judged it neceſſary to aſſume a title no human being envied, or offered to diſpute with me; and to ſupport it properly without encroaching on my daughter's valuable acquiſition, I found that I muſt reſolve to re-viſit Kenilworth Caſtle, now the property of another family.—In the building were contained cabinets ſo ſecure and unknown, that Lord Leiceſter always depoſited there, ere he journeyed to London, ſuch papers, jewels, and other valuables, as he thought it unſafe to take with him. On the memorable night when laſt we quitted that pleaſant dwelling, I had aſſiſted him to place in the moſt curious of theſe reſervoirs ſeveral caſkets, for which he ſeemed more than commonly anxious; and I added to their number, that containing Mrs. Marlow's papers, and the teſtimonials of my birth. As if actuated by ſome ſad pre-ſentiment that he ſhould never more re-viſit this ſpot, my Lord took great pains to familiarize me to the management of the ſprings, and gave into my hands duplicates of the keys. By a ſingular chance, amidſt all the tranſitions of my fate theſe keys remained, and ſeemed continually to remind me, how important to my daughter's welfare it might one day be to recover the caſkets.——Such a motive alone could conquer the reluctance I felt again to behold a ſpot ſacred to the memory of a huſband ſo beloved. You will call this perhaps, a childiſh weakneſs, after all I had borne; but alas, the mind feebler and feebler from every conflict, ſometimes ſinks under a trifle, after repelling the more powerful attacks of ill-fortune with magnanimity.

Lady Arundell, with her uſual kindneſs, propoſed accompanying me; and we ſorrowfully meaſured once more thoſe miles which ſo ſtrongly revived in my mind the moſt intereſting remembrances. At Coventry we reſted to inquire into the character of the preſent owner of Kenilworth Caſtle. We were told that this magnificent manſion, which I had left fit for the reception of a Sovereign, had long been in the hands

of

of a miser, whose avarice had induced him to strip it of its princely ornaments; not less from the desire of converting those into money, than to deprive it of every charm that might tempt the enquiring traveller to knock at the inhospitable gate. Yet, even when this ruin was effected, the structure itself remained so complete a piece of architecture as to attract a number of unwelcome visitors; to exclude whom, he had now let it to some manufacturers, and resided himself in a remote apartment. The chagrin this extraordinary revolution could not but occasion in my mind, was increased when I recollected how hard it would be, perhaps, to gain admission; and even when that was obtained, we knew not whether the only room I wished to lodge in was now habitable. Lady Arundell, with her usual foresight, advised me to seem to have no other motive for this visit, than a desire to re-purchase the Castle; and when shewn through it, to appear to be struck with so severe an indisposition, as soon as I reached the

chamber

chamber which contained the cabinets, as ſhould render it impoſſible to remove me; leaving it to her to reconcile the owner to ſo troubleſome an intruder, by the moſt laviſh generoſity. A fineſſe of this kind alone could aſcertain me any ſucceſs, and the ſickline\ſs of my aſpect, I was ſure, would ſufficiently corroborate ſuch an aſſertion.

We ſet out immediately, that by arriving in the evening we might have a pretence for paſſing the night there.—My ſoul turned from the well-known ſcene, and ſickened alike at ſight of the reviving verdure, and the ſplendid manſion, to me alas, only a gay mauſoleum. Humbly I ſolicited entrance at a gate which once flew open whenever I appeared; but, ah, though the exterior was the ſame, how ſtrange ſeemed the alteration within!—No more did the liveried train of aſſiduous domeſtics aſſemble to the diſtant winding of the huntſman's horn.—No longer did I reſt in gilded galleries, whoſe pictured ſides delighted one ſenſe, while their coolneſs refreſhed

another.

another. No longer could I, even in idea, behold the beloved, the noble owner, whoſe gracious mien endeared the welcome it conveyed—A change which jarred every feeling had taken place. A numerous body of diligent mechanics were plodding in thoſe halls in which Elizabeth had feaſted, and then battered ſides hardly now informed us where the rich tapeſtry uſed to hang. My ears were ſuddenly ſtunned with the noiſe of a hundred looms; and the diſtant lake once covered with gay pageants, and reſounding only to the voice of pleaſure, preſented us another ſcene of induſtry not leſs buſy, ſtrange, and ſurpriſing. By incidents of this kind, one becomes painfully and inſtantaneouſly ſenſible of advancing into life. When firſt we find ourſelves ſailing with the imperceptible current of time, engroſſed either by the danger of our ſituation, or enchanted with its proſpects, we glide ſwiftly on, ſcarce ſenſible of our progreſs, till the ſtream reviſits ſome favorite ſpot: alas, ſo viſible will be the deſolation of the ſhorteſt interval, that we grow

grow old in a moment, and ſubmit once more to the tide, willing rather to ſhare the ruin than review it.

Among the few ſervants retained by the meagre maſter of this deſolated manſion, one appeared who immediately recalled himſelf to my mind by the name of Gabriel. I recollected his having been warden of the outer lodges. The title by which I was announced—the weed I ſtill continued to wear, overcame a wretch already bowed to the earth by age, infirmity, and penury: and when to theſe circumſtances was ſuperadded the remembrance of the plentiful and peaceful days he had known under a Lord ever munificent to his domeſtics, gratitude became agony, and the poor old man ſunk in a fit at my feet. An incident like this might well have affected an indifferent ſpectator.—I was ſcarce more ſenſible than himſelf: and the alarm ſoon ſpread through the laborious mechanics, till it was conveyed to Sir Humphry Moreton.—Timorouſly he emerged from

his

his apartment, and, as the humble crowd made way for him, he measured me afar off with his eye, and seemed lost in conjecture on the subject of my visit.—My purse was yet in my hand, and part of its contents in those of some persons who had lent a ready assistance. Whether this, or the wan delicacy of my looks interested him, I know not; but every care-furrowed feature gradually relaxed as he approached me, striving in vain to soften into the smile of benevolence. I rose to return his courteous salutation, and informed him, that when last I passed the walls of this Castle, I was its mistress, the dear and happy wife of Lord Leicester; but perceiving uncertain apprehensions of some remote claim began again to contract his brow, I added, that sensible I had lost every right in a spot yet dear to me, I came to inquire whether he was disposed to part with it, and to rescue from poverty such worthy servants of its late noble owner as had alike outlived their labour, and him who should have recompensed it.

 What

What heart is insensible to that virtue in which we alone can resemble our Maker?——Benevolence, like religion, awes even those it cannot win. The miser loudly applauded my liberality. and by a greater effort on his part, allowing for the difference of our characters, invited me to spend the night in the Castle. The chamber I had been accustomed to inhabit he called his best, and thither was I conducted; I was not unprovided with the means of ensuring my own welcome, and my servants having spread the cold viands they brought, Sir Humphry's spirits grew light over luxuries he was not to pay for. A temptation so agreeable prolonged his stay, and I at length discovered that the only way to shorten his visit, would be to compliment him with all that remained: seeing my servants, in compliance with the hint, were about to convey it out of the room, fear lest any should be lost by the way, prevailed over the hilarity

of

of the moment, and he departed with the wine.

With an impatient beating heart I raiſed the tapeſtry, which providentially had been preſerved in this room, leſs from its beauty than antiquity; as it was ſo worn that it had long been pannelled in many places.—Behind the bed we diſcovered the ſecret ſpring of the cabinet, which I opened without any difficulty; and with the aſſiſtance of Lady Arundell took down the well-remembered caſkets, pauſing at intervals, to weep over all the tender ideas the ſight of them recalled ſo forcibly to my memory; then raiſing my eyes toward Heaven, while devoutly thanking the God who thus proſpered my remaining wiſhes, I almoſt fancied I beheld the beatified ſpirit of him who concealed theſe treaſures.

Lady Arundell would not reſt without inſpecting their contents. The largeſt was filled with family papers, bonds, contracts, mortgages, many of which were to me unintelligible, and all uſeleſs.

The

The next contained letters and little ornaments, leſs precious from their intrinſic value, that their analogy to particular events—under theſe was a gilt caſket filled with jewels, and what was infinitely more valuable, the authenticated bonds and acknowledgments of all the ſums Lord Leiceſter had providently depoſited in other countries; and of which I knew not that any memorandum remained. This was ſo noble an addition to the bequeſt which already enriched my ſweet Mary, that it ſeemed to me, as if her father even from the grave delighted to endow her: while the Almighty, gracious even when we think him moſt ſevere, had thus ſecreted, for her advantage, treaſures it would have been impoſſible for me to have preſerved through ſo many deſperate viciſſitudes.

The next caſket was a gift from the fond mother to the darling of her heart: it contained all the teſtimonials of the Queen of Scots, and other parties concerned

cerned on the ſubject of my birth, with the contract of marriage between Lord Leiceſter and myſelf. I felt rich in theſe recovered rights: and though prudence might never permit me to claim alliance with King James, yet to bequeathe to my daughter the power of doing ſo, at whatever period it ſhould appear advantageous, was a great conſolation to me.

Lady Arundell and I paſſed part of the night in packing theſe valuables in empty trunks brought for that purpoſe; then, cloſing the ſecret cabinet, and leaving no traces of our ſearch for it, we retired to reſt. We departed early the next morning, carrying with us that ancient domeſtic of Lord Leiceſter, on whom memory had ſo powerfully operated, and two others, who, long ſince expelled from the Caſtle, ſought a miſerable ſubſiſtence in the hamlets around it. It joyed my very heart to ſupply to theſe poor wretches a loſs irremediable with reſpect to myſelf, and the profound attachment of their few remaining days amply rewarded me.

Through the intervention of the friends I yet possessed, some eminent merchants in London undertook to get the bonds, notes, &c. duly acknowledged: and, in process of time, such considerable sums were of consequence recovered, as ascertained to myself and child our accustomed affluence. Years and misfortune had only cemented the ancient friendship between me and Lady Arundell.—I added my income and family to hers.——Her house was fortunately so near London as to allow me the advantage of procuring the first instructors for my daughter; and the infirm state of Lady Arundell's health, rendering her as much a prisoner from necessity, as I was from choice, both insensibly found, in the improvement of my daughter, a mild and growing satisfaction, which more than made amends for the world we shut out.

Ah! could I desire a greater pleasure? Pardon, madam, the fond extravagance

of

of maternal love, and allow me to present to you the darling of my heart in her sixteenth year. Already something taller than myself, to a form that united the strictest symmetry with the wild and variable graces of glowing youth, my Mary added the perfect features of her father, exquisitely feminized by a complexion transparently fair, and a bloom alike delicate and vivid; her hair, of the golden brown I have described as peculiar to his, fell below her waist in a profusion of artless ringlets, heightening her beauty even to luxuriance.—If she had borrowed any thing from me, it was the collected modesty of her mien; and from my sister she had stolen that penetrating, fascinating smile, those two alone of all I ever saw were gifted with:—alas, it was now wholly her own.—Although lightness and elasticity characterized her figure, every limb was rounded even to polishing, and never did I contemplate the soft turn of her white arms when raised to touch the lute, without thinking those more perfect than even her face.—Her voice was no less ſweet in ſpeaking than ſinging; with this difference—that in the firſt ſhe ſoftened the ſoul to pleaſure, in the laſt, elevated it to rapture.—Her underſtanding was ſtrong and penetrating, yet delicate and refined.—Her ſenſibility (the firſt formed of all her feelings) was rather deep than ardent. Maternal experience had moderated the enthuſiaſm incident to youth, nor was it obvious in any inſtance but the love of knowledge. Inceſſant, unremitting, in her ſtudies, books were her only extravagance, and muſick her only relaxation. To compenſate for the worldly pleaſures I judged it prudence to deprive her of, I was laviſh in thoſe to which her taſte naturally led: I kept muſicians on purpoſe to accompany her, and found, in the years filled up by herſelf and her employments, that ſweet though ſaddened pleaſure parents only know, and which, perhaps, more than makes us amends for all the lively ones it recalls to our memory.

memory. In effect, the more lovely she grew, the more necessary I found it to hide her; and, offering her daily up to God, I left her wholly to his disposal; determined neither my pride, vanity, or ambition, should interfere with the happiness I supplicated for her.

On perusing this description, I perceive at once the impossibility of your crediting it; yet, far from accusing myself of partiality, I could call on all who ever beheld my daughter to attest my candor.—How readily would Lady Arundell have done so—entendered to her by a love only inferior to my own, that faithful friend found in declining life a new tye wound round her heart, for which she daily thanked me.

As nothing robs us of the confidence of youth like the appearance of mystery, when time called reflection to being in her tender mind, I slowly and by degrees confided to my daughter the painful events you have thus obliged me to commemorate. This indulgence secured to me her whole heart, and I trembled only left her deep ſenſe of paſt misfortunes ſhould affect her health; for ſenſibility was the leading feature in her character. Far, however, from ſeeking to expound the future in her own favor, the flattering proſpects her diſtinguiſhed birth, and yet more diſtinguiſhed endowments, might well ſpread before her, paſſed away like a ſhadow, and ſhe ſaw only her mother. A thouſand times has ſhe bedewed my hand with a reverence the moſt endearing: and the tears with which ſhe often embalmed the memory of her father, almoſt recompenſed me for his loſs. From that period her expreſſive eyes were fixed ever on mine with ſuch blended ſadneſs and admiration, as proved ſhe thought me almoſt ſainted by misfortune. More ſtudious henceforward of my pleaſure, more ſubmiſſive to my will, more ſolicitous for my repoſe, it ſeemed as if, in learning that ſhe was my only remaining tye on earth, ſhe conceived that the various affections and duties of all I had lost devolved to, and centred in, herself. But sympathy was the genuine impulse of her nature; for with equal care she watched over her unhappy aunt.—Whenever that dear creature's incurable malady assumed the appearance of melancholy, she was extravagantly fond of musick.—At those intervals my lovely Mary would lean over her lute with the meek benignity of a descending angel, and extract from it such solemn sounds as breathed at once of peace and sorrow: insensibly soothing the perturbed spirit, and melting only those yet undisturbed. That subtle essence of our natures, sensibility, which madness can only unfix, not annihilate, often paused unconsciously upon the pleasure, and softly sunk into repose.

A child thus eminently amiable at once concentred my affections—commanded my esteem—possessed my whole confidence—actuated, in short, my very being.—Ah, how noble, how affecting is the friendship grounded on the maternal and filial tye; when, unconſcious of any weakneſs in her own heart, the mother dares preſent it as a pure and unflattering mirror to her child, and, with that ſelf-applauſe which even Heaven approves, contemplates the upright, the innocent ſoul it reflects! Sacred and indelible becomes that precept which is expreſſed but by example.—Happy are thoſe enabled to form ſuch an attachment as inexperience ſtrengthens on one hand, and knowledge on the other:—Neither the guſts of youthful paſſion, nor the nipping froſts of age, can deſtroy a plant rooted thus by mutual virtue;—it only gains vigor from time, and, by the peculiar indulgence of the Almighty, our ſublimeſt merit ripens into our moſt perfect pleaſure.

Satisfied that I had already acquired ſuch an influence in my daughter's mind as ſhould enable me to regulate her principles, I left it to years and circumſtances to call them into action.—The great buſineſs of my life now ſeemed over; and,

and, delivering my heart up to the flattering presages of maternal love, a thousand visions of almost forgotten grandeur and happiness floated before my eyes, and sometimes half-deluded them.

The fluctuating complaints of Lady Arundell at length settled into a consumption;—it was an hereditary disorder of the Sydneys: nor perhaps could the solicitude of myself and my sweet Mary have availed aught toward her restoration, even if a cruel shock, in which we were all equal sufferers, had not precipitated her fate.

Among the unconscious caprices which by turns actuated my unfortunate sister, was a passion for sitting in the open air.—Neither times or seasons had any influence over her; and she would insist on it alike in the snow of December, and the scorching sun of July.—To this self-will I had no doubt greatly contributed. From the moment of my return to England, I had vehemently opposed the severe controul to which she had heretofore

fore been ſubject, and habituated her attendants to yield to her in every inſtance which did not abſolutely endanger her ſafety; fully determined not to render an exiſtence wholly wretched no human being could now make happy. But as uninformed minds never know a medium, the people appointed to watch her gradually ſuffered her to become ſenſible of her power, which ſoon grew into an unbounded indulgence. It was now the depth of winter, and ſhe had ſat in the keen air for hours, watching the ſnow, which fell in abundance.——The moſt violent ſhiverings enſued, followed by a fever which ſettled at laſt on the nerves, and brought her to the very verge of the grave.—Nevertheleſs, it appeared to have ſalutary effects—her ſpirits were ſunk indeed to extreme lowneſs, but they became more equal, and traces of reaſon were often diſcernible in her actions. If ſhe did not remember, ſhe yet ſtrove to know me; and ſometimes ſtudied my features in a manner the moſt touching.

touching.—I confidered thefe efforts as the very crifis of her fate—her only chance on this fide Heaven, and fcarce dared leave her for a fingle moment. I entrufted the care of Lady Arundell (whofe fituation, though more dangerous, was not fo melancholy) to my daughter, fearful left her youthful fpirits fhould be injured by conftantly contemplating an object fo affecting. But I had forgot that my own fhattered conftitution was not equal to the fatigue and anxiety of watching over my fifter. I fell one evening into a fucceffion of fainting fits; the fervants conveyed me to bed; and the fear of alarming Lady Arundell hindered them from informing my daughter of my fituation My faintings at length gave place to a drowfinefs, fo intenfe that I might call it a ftupor.—I remained thus for fome hours, when I ftarted with an indiftinct idea of a heavy fall, and a deep groan. Terror roufed, and collected in a moment, every dormant faculty.—I rufhed through the chamber which divided mine from my fifter's, but I blamed myfelf for impetuofity

tuofity when I perceived that all was profoundly filent in hers. The two nurfes were in a deep fleep, and the expiring watchlights heavily winked, and revived, before the cold dawn of the morning. I gently opened the curtains of her bed—Ah, gracious Heaven, what did I feel when I beheld it empty!—The agonized fhriek I gave, rouzed both her carelefs attendants, who, impreffed with but one idea, flew towards a door I now firft perceived to be open: it led to a gallery ornamented with fuch portraits of our family as had furvived the wreck of their fortunes; among them had been incautioufly placed that (already fatally commemorated) of the Earl of Effex at the ftorming of Cadiz, an unfortunate legacy bequeathed to my fifter by Lady Pembroke.—My foul took in at a thought all the fearful confequences,—I tottered into the gallery—alas only to behold my worft apprehenfion verified.—The fair fpectre, which once was Ellinor, lay proftrate before the picture—one hand had convulfively gathered her difordered

garments

garments over her thin cheſt; the other was ſtill expreſſively extended towards the inanimate image of him ſo beloved—Impatiently I laid my hand upon her heart—it anſwered not the trembling inquirer—its wandering eſſence was exhaled, and ſhe had ceaſed for ever to ſuffer. Thy parting prayer, oh Eſſex! was ſurely prophetic, for her ſoul, in recovering memory, had burſt its mortal bound and ſoared to Heaven.

Scarce were the dear remains quietly interred, ere thoſe of the amiable Lady Arundell followed them. I bore theſe loſſes with devout reſignation——The tears which fall when Heaven recalls the unfortunate, ſtill the wild paſſions of the ſad ſurvivor, and deeply wound only the ſoul yet new to ſuffering. It was with a quickened apprehenſion that I perceived the effect of theſe firſt afflictions on the tender ſpirits of my daughter: not that I ſought totally to ſtifle the lively impreſſions of natural affection;—the tears of youth, like the genial ſhowers of

May,

May, ſerve only to ſave the planter's toil, and ſimply ripen the rich fruits of the mind; but when either fall too often, they impoveriſh the ſoil, and waſh away the buds yet blowing.

My own ſoul afforded no variety of cheerful images with which I could hope to invigorate the gentle ſpirits of my Mary: unwilling to form new connections, I rather thought it prudent to change my abode, and by a variety of ſcenes inſenſibly amuſe her; and my ſteward was ſent accordingly to ſeek another manſion. I recollected the moment when the gloomy aiſles of a ruined convent, by poſſeſſing the ſimple advantage of novelty, diverted my mind even at the ſorrowful criſis which robbed me of a foſter mother. Alas, in yet untried youth, the proſpect that is unknown ever adds to its own charms thoſe of imagination; while in maturer life, the heart lingers on all which once delighted it, hopeleſs of finding in the future, a pleaſure fancy can ever compare with thoſe it reviews in in the paſt. To my daughter, however, the whole world was yet new, and, in fixing on a ſcene habitual to my feelings, I could not fail to delight hers. I hired a manſion near the Thames ſide, in Richmond, to which we removed early in the ſpring.

Perhaps, in this choice, I was influenced, almoſt without knowing it, by a latent motive: diſtinct as I had lived from the world ſince my return to England, the fame of the Prince of Wales had yet reached me.—This accompliſhed youth had at once roſe above the weakneſſes of his father, and the prejudices of his rank; devoting his heart to the virtues, his mind to the ſciences, and his perſon to thoſe manly and becoming exerciſes which, invigorating every human power, prepared him alike for the enjoyment of peace, or the purſuit of war. Delighted to underſtand a Stuart was riſing to redeem the glory of his declining race, I paſſionately longed to ſee, know, and be valued by the royal

Henry.

Henry. The King, unworthy a ſon ſo diſtinguiſhed, took no pleaſure in his company; but, even in tender youth, reſigned him to a court of his own, from the adulation of which merit ſuperior to praiſe alone could have guarded him. Henry had, like myſelf, a partiality for the beautiful village of Richmond, he always paſſed part of the ſummer in a palace near the Thames; and I took pleaſure in thinking a partition of wood alone ſeparated his gardens from mine. With a judgment unequalled at his years, the Prince knew how to be affable without abating aught of his dignity; and, while in the circle of his own court he preſerved the authority of a ſovereign, to the unfortunate who addreſſed him, he had the benignity of a brother: ſuch was his character in Richmond, where the people almoſt adored him, and took pleaſure in amplifying on the ſuperior qualities he ſo eminently poſſeſſed. The ſweet hopes his merit ſometimes infuſed into

into my bosom, came accompanied with an equal number of fears, yet could not my heart forbear to cherish them.

The revolving season tinged this sweet retreat with every variety of verdure; the waves of the Thames were more translucent than ever; all nature awakened once more to perfection, when the Prince of Wales took up his abode in the adjacent palace.—This news heightened the soft red of my daughter's cheek, and even faintly coloured my wan one.—Not daring to express to her the eager desire I felt to see the Prince, and not accustomed to venture out without her, day after day elapsed in anxious expectation. My gentle Mary, with a delicacy from which I drew the most happy presages, now always chose to go abroad either so early or so late that it was almost impossible we should ever meet the Prince, and the veil she usually wore was closed with so much care as to ensure her the happiness of being overlooked, even if fortune threw him in our way.

Neverthelefs, I took notice that the arrival of the Royal Henry ftrangely filled up the void in our lives.—What he would do, or what he would not do, conftantly regulated our motions, and employed my daughter's thoughts even more than my own. His tafte afforded us a variety of indulgences of which he knew not that we were partakers.—Sometimes moon-light concerts, or magnificent fireworks; at others, parties on the Thames; where the Prince ftill took pleafure in beholding a variety of little veffels, built and ornamented for the amufement of his early years, and which were manned by children.—They were often fo near, that we fancied we heard the voice of Henry, when both mother and daughter would give way to the fame impulfe, and haftily retire. The fummer might have elapfed in this manner, had not chance been more favorable to our wifhes, than we could refolve to be.

We were returning home one morning in an ill-contrived carriage, newly invented

vented for airings, the inconvenience of which I bore patiently, from not being able to walk or ride on horseback for any length of time since my memorable fever.—The servant who drove stopt as usual at the brow of the inchanting hill, that we might enjoy for a few minutes its beauties, when the sound of horns approaching near, informed us that the Prince of Wales was returning from hunting, which at once startled the horses and ourselves. My Mary, actuated only by the impression of the moment, made an eager sign to the man to drive on; and the horses, already frightened, yielded impetuously to the slightest touch of the rein, flying forward with the most dangerous rapidity. The clumsiness of the carriage, and the badness of the road, threatened us every moment with being overturned—for me there was no escape; but could my daughter be prevailed on to leap out, I was sensible she would be safe. Far from obeying my intreaties, or even commands, she threw her arms around me, and protested it was for me alone she feared. The carriage sunk into a deep rut at last, and we were thrown out at a small distance, with a violence that almost deprived me of my senses:—my darling Mary had wholly lost hers.—I perceived the train of Henry approaching, but the favorite wish of seeing him was forgotten in that of recovering her.——I was presently environed by the hunters without regarding them, till their extreme solicitude obliged me to raise my eyes from the lifeless face of my daughter in acknowledgment. I perceived with a surprise even that moment could not conquer, that on each side of me stood a young man, adorned with the order of the garter, and so distinguishingly handsome, that I knew not which was the Prince of Wales, but turned from the one to the other with an air of wildness and stupor.—My looks, however, made little impression on the strangers, their whole attention being fixed on the inanimate form of my daughter.—

ter.—In truth, fortune had contrived to ſhew her to the utmoſt advantage. I had thrown up her veil to give her air, and bared her beautiful hands and arms, poliſhed and white as Parian marble; the wild rings of her auburn hair played on her youthful face, as the yellow leaves of Autumn curl over a latter peach; whilſt every feature, formed with a truth which might bear the niceſt examination, perhaps only appeared more exquiſitely regular from the abſence of expreſſion; and even her figure and attitude (leaning on her mother's knees) preſented a perfect model for a ſculptor. The aſſiduities of the ſtrangers, together with my own, at length recalled her ſcattered ſenſes.—— She opened thoſe eyes ſo dear to me, and fixing them for a moment on the two ſtrangers, a roſy ſuffuſion alone proved ſhe ſaw them, with ſuch quickneſs did ſhe turn toward her mother; when beholding me to appearance unhurt, ſhe lifted her ſoul to heaven in a glance of gratitude, and throwing her arms round my neck, relieved her overcharged heart by weeping on my boſom. "An angel in mind as well as form!" exclaimed one of the ſtrangers; "aſſure me, madam," continued he, "that this terror is the only ill conſequence of my ſudden approach, or I know not how I ſhall forgive it to myſelf." This addreſs aſcertaining the Prince of Wales, he became the ſole object of my attention.——Ah, where ſhall I find words to endear to you, Madam, the royal youth my heart at once opened to adopt? Henry was yet but in the dawn of manhood, nevertheleſs his height was majeſtic, and his figure finiſhed. The beauty of his features was their leaſt charm—virtue herſelf ſeemed to ſublime every happy lineament, and ſpare beholders the trouble of developing his character by conveying it in a glance. His manly voice united the firmneſs of his own ſex with the ſenſibility of ours. A confuſion of ſad remembrances were at once preſented with him to my mind; and the admiration he excited

was

was ſtrangely blended with regret.—I forgot that he had addreſſed me, and continued to contemplate him in ſilence; ever and anon turning my ſtreaming eyes wildly from him to heaven, even then, my dilating heart bids me add, ſcarce changing the object. The amiable Henry, in whoſe nature ſympathy was the prevailing ſentiment, touched with a conduct ſo myſterious, almoſt forgot my daughter in turn, ſo wholly was he engroſſed by me.—Informed of my unfortunate lameneſs by my attempting to riſe, he immediately concluded it to be the conſequence of the recent accident, and ſcarce was ſatisfied by my aſſurances of the contrary. Oh! as my eyes ſurveyed the ſuperior ſoul, living, irradiated in the bright orbs of his, how did they ſtream at remembering that, had his father been born but to half his virtues, I might now have been cheriſhed by affection—dignified by rank—unwidowed—unbroken—a ſtranger yet to ſorrow!—My mother too—Moſt unhappy of parents as well as ſovereigns! I had a tear for thee at this interesting moment.

The respect due to strangers induced the Prince to conceal the curiosity my conduct could not fail to excite, but having informed himself from the attendants of my title, he addressed me by it, and insisted on conducting me home. I now understood the nobleman who had divided my first looks with the Prince, was the Viscount Rochester: that contemptible favorite of the King, celebrated only for his beauty.—The visible coldness of my air checked a forward insolence I observed in him, and obliged him to quit us on our arriving at home.

With what secret transport did my soul welcome a Stuart worthy that name, glorious for so many ages!—The Prince seemed delighted with his new acquaintances.——The soft reserve of my daughter's air——the deepening roses of her cheek, and the low accent of her harmonious voice, when politeness obliged her to answer the Prince, whose animated eyes reduced hers often to seek the ground, preſented to my elated heart every ſymptom of that paſſion which alone endears the ſufferings it occaſions. A flow of happy ſpirits, new to my daughter, almoſt forgotten by myſelf, gave cheerfulneſs to the hour which Henry ſaw elapſe with regret.

On this chance introduction was grounded an acquaintance a few days ripened into intimacy.—Led to diſtinguiſh the Prince alike by his own merit, and the ties of blood, which ſecretly allied me to him, it was with the tendereſt ſatisfaction I beheld Henry cheriſh the inclination he had already conceived for my daughter: yet the dignity of his mind forbidding him to form an engagement he knew not how to fulfil, it was through me alone he addreſſed himſelf to her. Convinced it was in my power to prove her entitled even to ſuch a lover, I ſuffered fate to take its courſe, attending only to prudence.

Conſcious that Henry had hitherto moved in a very confined circle, I was aware that to extend it muſt draw much obſervation

ſervation on thoſe he favored. To guard therefore againſt the malice of ſurmiſe, I fixed on the hour of the Prince's viſit for my daughter to ride out; and always received him alone. His attendants, who ſaw her regularly depart, were at a loſs to imagine what could attach their royal maſter to the infirm widow of Lord Leiceſter. The charm was in truth ſimply affection.—The amiable Henry had early been accuſtomed to every kind of homage but that of the heart, and had too much ſenſibility not to feel the want he knew not how to ſupply. Deeply ſuſceptible of the true regard I had conceived for him, impreſſed at once by my mind, my manners, and my mien, with the idea of myſtery, and the deſire of obtaining my confidence, it was only by his own candour he ſought to gain upon mine. Slowly and by degrees he deigned to repoſe with me thoſe regrets and anxieties from which the utmoſt indulgence of nature and fortune cannot exempt a ſingle individual. He often lamented the dangerous diſtinction of being the firſt-

born

born of his father's children, ſince it coſt him every other—Separated almoſt in infancy from his parents——ſurrounded with mercenary ſycophants, who ſought to make their court to the reigning King by a partial repreſentation or miſconſtruction of his actions, he had ſhot up unloved, uncheriſhed, and ſeen thoſe tender affections he was born to ſhare, gradually center in that ſon from whom his parents had nothing to fear.———Nor were there wanting inſidious flatterers equally ready to undermine his filial duty, by pointing out the weakneſſes of his father, even where they were moſt likely to wound him. He had puniſhed himſelf, he added, for yielding to theſe impreſſions by an abſolute obedience to the authority of the King, but it was with grief he remembered that was now the only tye between them.—Nor would I wonder, he continued, it ſhould be ſo, if I conſidered that, born as he was to imperial power, with an ardent paſſion for glory, he had hitherto been ſhut up in the narrow ſphere of his own court, languiſhing away the flower

flower of his youth, without a choice, a friend, or a pursuit.—till the infamous Carr should deign to decide what foreign Prince's bribe he would condescend to accept, and to what bigotted Papist he should sacrifice the son of his master.

While the admired Prince of Wales, the Idol of the people, the Heir of Empire, the endued of Heaven, thus confided to me the simple and rational griefs which clouded a fortune so brilliant, could I fail to meditate on the equality of Providence?—which graciously allots even to the lowest situation, some portion of happiness, and depresses the highest with the sad sense of misfortune.

It is the fatal peculiarity of youth to throw the strongest light on every secret grief, and waste away under an oppression imagination often doubles. To cure this propensity is therefore the province of experience. I sought to imbue the Prince's mind with the only principle mine had derived from all my sufferings.—That the noblest use we can make of

under-

understanding is to convert it into happiness; and that every talent which does not conduce to that great end, ought rather to be considered as a burthen than a blessing to the possessor.—That the mind, like the eye, ever magnifies the object of fear or aversion, which often, on a strict examination, excites no other sentiment than contempt.—In fine, that he was not at liberty to shew any other sense of his father's errors, than by presenting a faultless example in his own life; and that, if he would have it without blemish, he must divert his taste from channels where it would meet with opposition, and turn it into those through which it might flow freely.—That the cultivation of the sciences would at once fill up the void in life ever so painful at his years, and attach to his welfare all who loved them; a body whose influence was never known unless opposition called forth the powers of eloquence.

The

The Prince had too much judgment not to ſee the utility of this counſel, and too much generoſity not to value its candour: nevertheleſs, it was a language yet new to him.—Ingenuity had been exhauſted to teach him to govern others, but to ſubdue himſelf was a leſſon none had ventured to inculcate. How did I lament that a ſoul ſo ductile had in childhood been injudiciouſly delivered up to its own guidance, and ſuffered every day to imbibe ſome new prejudice, deſtined perhaps to mark the character through life; and which an upright and ſkilful monitor might ſo eaſily have eradicated!

The Prince could not be inſenſible to the maternal caution which induced me to ſend my daughter abroad whenever he honored me with a viſit, yet the obſervation did not for ſome time appear to influence his conduct.—Satisfied with merely beholding her as he entered or departed, the deſire of opening his heart to me ſeemed to ſuperſede every other impreſſion.

ſion. Nevertheleſs, long reveries would follow the moſt accidental meeting, and long pauſes intervene in the moſt intereſting converſation; rendering it ſufficiently obvious, that his mind labored with ſome project, hitherto ſuppreſſed either by pride or prudence.

Perhaps I ſhould ever have wanted courage to open my lips on ſo delicate an occaſion, had not my daughter complained to me that ſhe was now become the univerſal object of attention; and that the ſuit who attended her were often rudely ſurrounded, and ſometimes interrogated by ſuch of the Prince's court as had not benefited by his example.—By going abroad unexpectedly with her, I found that ſhe was not offended without reaſon, and ſenſible of my imprudence in thus riſquing her ſafety, I came to the reſolution rather to abridge myſelf of the pleaſure of the Prince's ſociety, than purchaſe it by endangering my daughter.———I deſired her to retire for awhile when Henry ſhould viſit me me next, and ere he could account for the ſingularity of finding her at home, entered into the delicate explanation. With an acknowledged attachment to him, that I bore my child alone could have over-ruled, I ſubmitted it to himſelf, whether I could too cautiouſly guard againſt a cenſure or inſult ſhe had no natural protector to reſent.—The generous Henry pauſed for a few moments with irreſolution, when ſuddenly collecting courage he broke ſilence.—"Will Lady Leiceſter pardon," ſaid he, "thoſe obtruſive viſits ſhe has ſubmitted to with ſo much complacency? Will ſhe deign to become the confidant of the only incident in my life I have hid from her—will ſhe liſten with indulgence?"—He pauſed a moment, but, ere I could reſolve how to anſwer, purſued the diſcourſe——"Accuſtomed even from childhood to the enſnaring glances of the light and the lovely—led to imagine myſelf older than my years by the continual propoſals for marrying me that have conſtantly ſucceeded each other, it is not wonderful that a heart naturally ſuſceptible ſhould mature before its time. Among the many beautiful girls, who have already ſought to attract me, I ſoon diſtinguiſhed one, by whom my peace, my honor, my innocence became endangered: perhaps they had been loſt, had I not found her ſelfiſh and ambitious. I need hardly inform you that this ſeducing fair one is the Counteſs of Eſſex!—Vain of her influence over me, ſhe took pleaſure in publiſhing it, and taught me early to bluſh for my choice; but I could not reſolve to do ſo continually. I formed the bold reſolution of contending with my own heart, and retired hither to recover it, or die. Lady Eſſex, enraged and humbled at this conduct, confirmed me in it, by attaching herſelf to Viſcount Rocheſter: thus rendering it ſufficiently obvious, ſhe had never loved me.—Beſotted with her beauty, that weak favorite is governed by her caprices, and him I was born to obey yields to thoſe of Rocheſter. Although

though I do not immediately perceive how Lady Eſſex means to effect her revenge, I am convinced that it is only maturing; and daily expect a blow, from which I know not how to guard myſelf. Under theſe circumſtances how can I venture to involve your fate with mine?—How can I aſk you to permit me to offer to your lovely daughter the heart which ever hovers near her?—Speak Madam—my happineſs is in your hands—dare you riſque your own to promote it?" While I liſtened to this ſenſible, this frank declaration of the Prince's error, and his attachment, my fond heart found its firſt wiſh accompliſhed, and adopted at once the royal youth; ſolemnly vowing to ſhare, without repining, every evil that might follow an alliance ſo dear: nor did I fail ſecretly to exult in my Mary's hereditary right even to this diſtinction.

To cement the confidence between us, and convince the prince that his preſent choice was judicious, I reſolved to confide to him the ſecret ſo long, ſo painfully preſerved;

ſeived; and related my whole hiſtory. As I retraced its affecting incidents, I knew them to be ſo only by his eager, his generous ſympathy; ſo wholly was my own ſoul engroſſed by the happy proſpect he had opened before it.

The Prince of Wales acknowledged with joy the relationſhip I claimed; and, to confirm all I had advanced, I offered him the long-ſaved teſtimonials, which he peruſed with ſilent reverence: then fixing his eyes, ſtill impreſſed with that elevated ſentiment, on mine, he gave utterance to the dictates of his heart.—"Who would ſuppoſe," exclaimed he, "a fortitude ſo unexampled could poſſibly be combined with a frame delicate even to fragility!—May the misfortunes you have indelibly impreſſed on my memory, my more than mother, be the laſt of your life—May that being who directed my ſoul to cheriſh the admiration and eſteem inſpired by your lovely daughter, and matchleſs ſelf, ſuffer the youth before you to ſupply to your heart, all it ought to have inherited—all it unhappily has loſt. Dear will be the moment when to the form of your angel mother my authority ſhall add the name, and that moment will hereafter, oh! moſt honored of women, infallibly be mine."

While I liſtened to predictions ſo flattering, I almoſt believed them accompliſhed. In thy unblown youth, oh, royal Henry, was compriſed every promiſe that could dilate or fill the heart: mine centred at once in thee, and my daughter: finding in the mere hope of ſo glorious a union, a total ſuſpenſion from ſuffering and ſorrow.

I had now no reſerves with the Prince, and leading in my bluſhing Mary preſented her to her royal couſin; who gracefully offered up his unblemiſhed ſoul on the hand he bowed over. So pure a tranſport took poſſeſſion of mine as obliterated every other impreſſion. I ſnatched the united hands ſo dear, ſo beloved, and preſſing them to my boſom, ſickened with very ecſtaſy, and withdrew to recover myſelf.—Wandering alone by the

the ſide of the Thames, I raiſed my full eyes to heaven; and called the happy ſpirits of my mother, ſiſter, and Lord Leiceſter, to ſympathize with me in an event which promiſed to end the perſecutions of my family, by thus bleſſedly uniting the laſt ſprung branches of it. A ſerenity of the ſublimeſt nature ſucceeded the ſweet trouble of my ſpirits, and enabled me to rejoin the youthful lovers with the dignity due to my own character.

The ſituation in which we ſtood endeared us ſtill more to the Prince, by perpetually reminding him how intimately our welfare was connected with his own. Every hour ſeemed to unite us more and more to each other. Henry ſpoke to me with the freedom of a ſon, conjuring me not to take any ſtep that would create the leaſt ſuſpicion of my birth, or the ſecret tye formed between us, till he had well weighed every conſequence that might enſue: and, to elude the watchful ſpies, with whom we were alike ſurrounded, he propoſed paſſing in the evening through his garden to ours, if I would deign for a while to allow him thus to reach the saloon. Our situation was too delicate not to require the strictest caution, yet as I could discover no mode of receiving the Prince, which was not equally questionable, and more dangerous, I acquiesced in his proposal, as well as that he should render one of his gentlemen (Sir David Murray) a confidant of this intimacy, though not of its nature, or extent.

An incident so important engrossing my every thought, my heart returned once more eagerly into the world. It had now an interest in fully understanding the real characters of the King, the Queen, Viscount Rochester, and every individual likely or intitled to interfere at this interesting crisis—I examined, considered, and weighed every thing. I soon discovered that the whole royal family were at variance! That the imperious Queen, unable to wrest her husband from his favorites, or her son from his duties, scorned the first, and neglected the latter; confining herself wholly to a

court

court formed of her own creatures, who assisted her to spoil her younger son; whom she had almost estranged from his brother. Her beautiful daughter, who united in her own person the graces of Mary with the spirit of Elizabeth, alone allured to the court of the Queen the few persons of merit it afforded. Henry was often lavish in the praises of his sister, and, as she was the only relation he ever voluntarily spoke of, I naturally concluded that she was the only one intitled by superior qualities to that distinction. King James, who had mounted the throne under happier auspices than almost any preceding sovereign of England, had already lived long enough to lose the affections of his people. By turns a pedant and a buffoon, his solemnity was even more disgusting than his levity. Governed by a predilection of the most absurd and singular nature, to a beautiful favorite he always delivered up the reins of empire; readily submitting to a shameful subjection in all important points, provided he might enjoy a ridiculous supremacy in his hours of indulgence and retirement. From ſuch a weak and inconſiſtent King, and his profligate Miniſters, the wiſe, the ſcientific, and the good, had gradually retreated; and, in neglect and ſilence, contemplated from far the growth of that exemplary Prince, who promiſed to retrieve the fame of his anceſtors, and the glory of the kingdom he was born to reign over. A youth of eighteen capable of uniting the unbleniſhed virtues of that age, with the diſcernment of a maturer one, was a phænomenon, and of courſe either adored or deteſted—While the body of the kingdom regarded the Prince of Wales only with the firſt ſentiment, the worthleſs favorites of his father were actuated ſolely by the latter.

To marry and eſcape the plans of Rocheſter was the intereſt of Henry; and to marry without his father's knowledge his unwilling choice.—Yet highly ſenſible of the ſlavery impoſed by his rank, he had reſiſted every temptation from beauties of an inferior one:—but, when apprized of my ſtory, he ſaw, or fancied he ſaw, in my daughter, a wife allotted him by heaven—one to whom no juſt objection could poſſibly be made; one born to give happineſs to his heart, and honor to his name. Nor could he doubt, even if his father ſhut his eyes againſt the truth, but that he ſhould be able to convince the people of my birth, when the publication of the marriage ſhould give my ſtory the whole weight of his credence.

Succeſs, in his judgment, depended ſolely on the concealment of the purpoſed union till it could be accompliſhed; for, if the intention tranſpired ere the event, he was ſatisfied the moſt deſperate efforts would be made to wreſt us from him. Yet as at this very period a public treaty was negociating with a foreign Prince, he could not form a tye of ſuch importance without giving his father juſt cauſe of offence, the nation at large a contempt for his character, and the diſtant Sovereign thus inſulted a mortal diſguſt. We therefore agreed to wait till this Miniſterial project like many others ſhould diſappoint itſelf, and ſeize that moment to

celebrate

celebrate and publiſh a marriage, which was to end all our fears, and complete all our hopes.

During this interval I obſerved with pain that the extreme timidity of my daughter's character prevailed over the enthuſiaſm incident to her years; and damped with vague apprehenſions thoſe moments love and hope might have made ſo happy. I ſaw this little feminine weakneſs with extreme uneaſineſs. The Prince of Wales was diſtinguiſhed by a manly firmneſs, which ever wiſely weighed the approaching trial, then calmly dared it. For a ſoul ſo noble, I deſired to find a faultleſs bride; and looking fearfully into the future, I ſometimes thought my Mary's timid heart would one day throb without cauſe againſt that of a ſovereign oppreſſed with innumerable cares, he perhaps ſought to loſe the remembrance of in her ſociety. Nevertheleſs, I did not perceive my tender admonitions on this ſubject had any other conſequence than that of inducing my daughter to bury in her boſom thoſe ſentiments and emo-

tions,

tions, I had ſo many years delighted to participate.

It was now autumn!——The time of the King's periodical progreſſes.——The Prince could not avoid following his father, but he lingered in his duty; and having ſtaid a day too long with us, haſtened to overtake the King, whom he was to feaſt at Woodſtock. He wrote to me from thence, complaining of fatigue and laſſitude; but, with his uſual attention, informed me that he was in treaty for Kenilworth Caſtle; where he flattered himſelf I ſhould again ſee golden days, like thoſe I ſtill remembered with ſo much pleaſure.

Alas, the few he had irradiated were quickly haſtening to a period! At the firſt viſit he paid me on his return, my ſoul was ſtruck with a very apparent alteration in his perſon; which was grown thin and wan beyond conception, conſidering the ſhortneſs of the time. Not all the joy he expreſſed at our meeting could ſatisfy me that he was either well or happy; but, obſerving he evaded my queſtions, and fearful of alarm-

ing

ing him without reaſon, I ſtrove to ſuppreſs that maternal anxiety which all his aſſurances of health and cheerfulneſs could not diſpel. I perceived my daughter was impreſſed with the ſame idea, for, though ſhe ſpoke not, it was viſible to me that ſhe wept greatly when alone.

The evenings were now too ſhort and damp for me to allow the evening viſits of the Prince; and I rather choſe to riſque every danger by receiving him openly, than ſubject him to any by an ill-judged caution.——Alas, theſe cares were vain.——The rapid decay of the royal Henry's health became viſible even to indifferent ſpectators. An affecting languor was the only expreſſion of thoſe fine eyes once ſo full of fire, and the youthful cheeks every following day ſhould have tinged with a deeper bloom, grew more and more wan and hollow—He could no longer conceal his illneſs. Alas, it pierced me to the ſoul! I was miſerable at remembering a charge ſo precious, as his welfare, ſhould be committed to ſervants of whatever denomination.

nation.—-No mother—-no ſiſter—-duties indiſpenſable in every other rank of life, were it ſeems incompatible with royalty. Oh, Henry!—dear amiable youth! even yet am I tempted to accuſe myſelf for not having better deſerved the tender appellation thy filial reverence ſo often beſtowed on me, by daring every thing for thy ſake! Slaves to imperious cuſtom, our actions are too often regulated by that idle multitude, whoſe moſt laviſh applauſes would but ill conſole us for one ſingle reproach from that unerring monitor, our own conſcience.

Either not convinced that this ſecret malady was undermining his conſtitution, or indifferent to the event, the Prince ſtill continued in the purſuit of his uſual athletic exerciſes and habits, till his ſtrength became wholly unequal to them. I once more perſuaded him to call in medical aſſiſtance, and he promiſed to attend to himſelf as ſoon as his ſiſter and the elector ſhould depart.—Obliged to appear at the celebration of their marriage in London, he came to pay us a parting viſit.

fit. Impressed, perhaps, with the idea that it would be the last, he threw himself into my arms, and shed there the first tears I had ever seen fall from his eyes.—Mine readily overflowed—a grief too deep for utterance pressed upon my soul, and Henry recovered ere I could. His heart missed my daughter, who was gone abroad.—He sighed, sunk into a little reverie, and breaking it, with a faint smile, said, "he ought rather to congratulate himself on her absence." He sighed again, and, after another pause, resumed his discourse in a low and broken voice.—"Mourn not thus, my mother (for I will still give you a title you may justly claim from her who bore me; since who ever loved me as you have done?) I have youth in my favor, and this oppressive malady may not be mortal: for your sake alone do I wish it to be otherwise, believe me.—Already weary, disgusted with this world, I could retreat from it almost without a pang, did I not know my loss would be to you an irremediable calamity. Yet who shall judge of the dispensations

of

of the Almighty ?—I might fulfil all your wifhes without feeing you happy—I might obtain all my own without ceafing to be wretched. Recall this often to your memory, whatever follows our parting, and remember your name will be ever on thefe lips while they have power to utter a found.—For the adored of my foul—but fhe is furely become a part of it; and if not permitted to poffefs her in this world, I will expect her in a better."—Perceiving his dim eye was fixed on a picture of my daughter which hung at my bofom, I prefented it to him.——"And do you too, beloved Henry," returned I, in a broken voice, "remember that the mother who gives you this, would have comprifed in the original every grace, every virtue, to be found through human nature: and having done fo, would ftill have thought her honoured in your choice.—Ah! royal youth! refign not a heart fo noble to vapourifh depreffion.—Your life, your happinefs, are not your own merely—a nation is born to pray for the former, to crown you with the latter.—For myſelf—upon the ſweet hope of matching my daughter with you, of ſharing the ſoft tranſports of mutual virtue and affection, I have learnt to live, but ſurely I could never ſurvive its extinction."—My full ſoul allowed not of another ſyllable. The Prince fixed his ſuffuſed eyes on mine, with a myſterious melancholy, almoſt amounting to deſpair, and touching with his lips thoſe hands his trembling ones ſtill graſped, ruſhed precipitately into the court yard. The ſound of his voice drew me towards the window——the graceful youth made me a laſt obeiſance and galloped away; while my partial eye purſued him till beyond its reach, and even then my ear ſeemed to diſtinguiſh the feet of his horſe.

With his uſual kind conſideration Henry wrote to me the next day, that he found himſelf better; and, in the pleaſure of ſeeing his ſiſter happy, felt reconciled to the impolitic match made for her.—He even aſſiſted at the various feſtivals with which the nuptials of the royal Elizabeth were honored; but ſcarce were they over, when his health and ſpirits failed at once, and the faculty were called in to his aid. A malady which had been ſo long engrafting itſelf on his conſtitution, left but little hope of his life;—I had ceaſed to entertain any: yet, far from ſupporting the idea of loſing him with fortitude, my ſoul mourned as if it then had firſt known ſorrow. Not daring to give free vent to my apprehenſions in the preſence of my daughter, I ſtrove with cold and watery ſmiles to flatter thoſe hopes in her heart my own had long rejected, and ſaw with vain regret, the deep exceſſes of a ſenſibility I had laboured to excite and ſtrengthen.

What days, what nights of ſadneſs and ſuſpenſe were ours, while the unfortunate Henry was languiſhing away every vital power ere yet they had reached maturity!—Frequently delirious, our names eſcaped unconſciouſly from thoſe lips, which at his lucid intervals, uttered only ſighs and groans. Murray, his beloved attendant, gave us conſtant information of the progreſs of his fever; nor did the amiable Henry fail at intervals to charge him with tender remembrances. Sir David at length acquainted me that, as the impassioned delirium of the Prince pointed ever toward us, the King had been apprized of it,—that he had minutely questioned his son's most favoured attendants, and among them himself, on the origin, progress, and strength, of an attachment thus suddenly and strangely brought to light, deeply ruminating on all he heard "I could not feel acquitted to myself, madam," concluded the faithful Murray, "were I to conceal this, nor dare I add a surmise on so delicate an occasion."

"Ah, of what importance to us are all the late inquiries, the vague conjectures of James!" cried I, folding my daughter to my bosom, "if heaven deprives us of his inestimable son, neither his love or his hatred can greatly affect us.—Beloved Mary—dear inheritor of misfortune!—widowed ere yet thou art a wife, a long obscurity, a solitary youth is all thy portion—a sorrow which can never end thy mother's—But why should I hesitate to avow myself?—Wherefore should I not publish claims which even tyranny cannot cancel, but perhaps it will not dispute? The timid, abject spirit of James knows not how to contend with one firm in virtue—immutable in truth.—Ah, had I done so long since, I might at this moment, dear Henry, have hovered near thy couch, and softened the anguish no mortal can prevent!—Perhaps the King already surmises the fact—let him demand it."

Sir David Murray's next letter breathed the very spirit of despair.———"Prepare yourself, madam," said he, "for the worst; perhaps, ere this reaches you, England will have lost its dearest hope, the royal Henry's friends their only one. The most desperate efforts of art have failed, and exhausted reason often now revisits with a languid ray the noble heart she is so soon to quit for ever. The Prince has just ordered me to commit to the flames every letter and paper in which you are mentioned :—a sure proof that he has given himself up.—Alas, he knows not how often names so dear have escaped him ; he has called for you, madam, and your angelic daughter, almost the whole night, but frequently recollecting himself, has waved his feeble hand, and sighed out no——no——no."

Three hours after, another express arrived.——"Pardon, madam, the haste and incoherency of scrawls penned at so trying a moment.—Alas, the most sanguine of the household has now ceased to hope.—Our royal master's speech entirely fails him—his last effort was hastily and repeatedly to call me—I flew to his bedside ; but, though my every sense seemed to resolve into ear, I found it impossible to understand him—either I widely erred or he named France ; perhaps I commit a second error in supposing he referred to you, madam, but I voluntarily risque every thing to fulfil the parting wish of a master so adored. The King, the physicians, all have taken a long leave of the

the almoſt beatified Prince; and there is nothing left for thoſe who love him beſt to wiſh, but that his pure ſpirit may paſs away in peace."

The agony and ſtupor this affecting billet occaſioned, were hardly abated when another arrived.——"It is all over, madam," concluded the worthy Murray, "raiſe your ſtreaming eyes to heaven; it is there alone you can now look for the incomparable Prince of Wales.—Fatigue and anguiſh diſable me from ſaying more."

It was not till the awful moment which reſtored the unſullied ſoul of Henry to its omniſcient Creator, that I had dared to breathe a wiſh of which he was not the object, or allowed my thoughts to paſs beyond himſelf.—That exquiſite ſenſibility which lives through all dear to us, had made me ſeverely ſuffer with him, and conſequently pray for that releaſe which alone ſeemed likely to give him eaſe; nor did I recollect till he was gone for ever, the void his loſs would leave in my hopes.—The tremendous calm, by which death is ever followed, now took its turn. Bereft of a ſupport on which I had long unconſciouſly reſted, I ſunk into a deſolation which made me almoſt wiſh to follow the lamented Prince.—It is at theſe intervals, madam, we become moſt truly ſenſible of all the imperfections of our nature.—How often had I flattered my own erring heart with the vain belief that it had acquired ſtrength, purity, and virtue, from its various trials! alas, what but pride, vanity, and ambition, ſtill throbbed unalterably there! time had only altered the object, not the paſſion, and centred them all in my daughter.

We ſhut ourſelves entirely up, and deeply joined in the general mourning. The ſad pleaſure of knowing him we bewailed, univerſally lamented, was yet ours. I peruſed, I appropriated, with a mother's fondneſs, the laviſh eulogies, all ſects, all parties, all poets, graced the memory of the Prince with.—it was the only mi-

mitigation my grief could know.—A considerable time had elapsed without our hearing any thing from Murray, in confirmation of his conjecture concerning Henry's last wish, and the imperfect accents which lingered on his dying lips.—But though I could not resolve to become a guiltless fugitive even in compliance with Prince Henry's will, I had had no other motive for remaining in England than to shew that I was not driven out of it. I now determined to quit a country which had been the grave of a hope so dear, and found my daughter entirely of my mind. In gratitude for the unwearied attention of Sir David Murray, I informed him "of my intention to retire into Flanders, not doubting but that the Hollanders would afford an honorable asylum to the widow and orphan of Lord Leicester.—I besought him to accept a ring of considerable value in token of my deep sense of the generous attachment he had shewn alike to myself, and that incomparable Prince whose loss was ever present to my mind; and requested as a laſt proof of his regard, the reſtoration of that picture of my daughter I had given to the royal Henry at our memorable parting."

The anſwer of Murray ſtrangely ſtartled and alarmed me.——"Your intention of quitting England, madam," ſaid he, "relieves my mind from extreme anxiety;—time and circumſtances have united to convince me that I did not miſunderſtand the laſt imperfect accents of my much-loved maſter.—Loſe not a moment in haſtening to the aſylum you have fixed on.—The picture, madam, is, I fear, irretrievably gone—I cannot by either bribes or intreaties procure any tidings of it.—*Power*, alas, I now have not!—If ever it comes to my hands, rely on its being reſtored by him who will ever devoutly pray for your happineſs."

This inexplicable letter rouſed every dormant faculty.—Wherefore ſhould my retiring abroad relieve the mind of a perſon unconnected with me *from extreme anxiety?*——Why ſhould he urge thus my departure? As it was rather

pride

pride than prudence which induced me to seek a country where I might fearlessly assert my every right, that project was now rejected from the very motive which first dictated it.—A mystery my nature ever disdained. Resolved to comprehend all the motives on which Murray wished me to act, I ordered every thing to be replaced, and sat down once more quietly at home; resolved to brave the storm, if indeed there was any gathering, rather than ascertain my safety by a disgraceful flight. I once more wrote to Sir David, acquainting him with my present conduct, and its reasons, insisting on being fully informed of those which actuated him to offer me advice so singular and mysterious.—How infinitely was my impatience, curiosity, and disdain, heightened by his answer!——"I hear with admiration, madam, a determination which from a perfect knowledge of your character, I ought, perhaps, to have foreseen; nevertheless, my sentiments are not altered, nor less urged, could I divulge the reaſons on which they are grounded: but decorum and delicacy give way to your commands, and the occaſion. Nevertheleſs, I find it impoſſible to commit them to paper.—Dare you give me admiſſion at midnight?—I ſhall be near your gate upon the chance, but be wary in the choice of my conductor, as perhaps my life, nay, even your own, depends upon its being ſuppoſed you never had any private correſpondence or communication with me."

How did my nature take fire at this incomprehenſible letter!—Me to ſtoop to ſecrecy!—to be expoſed to ſhame!—The unknown danger, with which he repreſented me to be environed, appeared wholly indifferent; ſo exquiſitely ſenſible was my ſoul of the imputation of diſhonor.—At times I reſolved to ſhut out Murray, and leave the brooding miſchief to diſcloſe itſelf by its effects; but love for my daughter controlling the ſtrong ſpirit of indignation inſeparable from innocence, I yielded to the ſuggeſ-

tions

tions of prudence, and prepared to admit him.—Inured to every other ſpecies of ſuffering, I knew not how to bluſh before any human being.

My perplexed and agitated mind paſſed through the infinitude of poſſibilities without fixing upon one.—At times I imagined all the caution of the royal Henry had been inſufficient, and that the King, by means of ſome loſt or ſecreted letter, had been fully apprized of his ſon's attachment to us, and the hopes that were grounded upon it; though even then I knew not why my life ſhould be in the queſtion; ſtill leſs could I imagine it endangered, had his diſcoveries reached farther, and traced out the long buried ſecret of my birth. Involved in buſy, vague, and alarming conjectures, I hardly knew how to wait with any patience for the ſingular hour appointed to aſcertain them.

Senſible, by the deep effect this took on my own mind, that it muſt dreadfully ſhock my daughter's, and ſtill flattering myſelf

myſelf that this indiſtinct danger might be the creation of a deſponding temper in Henry's favorite, I reſolved to wait the event of my midnight interview with Murray, ere I confided more to my Mary than ſhe muſt already have learnt from the change in my reſolution reſpecting quitting England.—But as to ſee her was to explain all, (for how could I hope to veil emotions which burnt indignantly on my cheek?) I ſent her word that I was ſeized with a violent head-ach, which I would endeavour to remedy by ſleep; and accompanied this meſſage with a new book ſhe had an eager deſire to ſee, and which I ſincerely prayed might wholly occupy her attention at this intereſting criſis.

Oh, world! how falſe, how erroneous are the feelings we imbibe from thee!—Nature ordained ſhame to be the companion of guilt, but overbearing cuſtom has broke that tye, and oftener bids her follow virtue. Scarce could I reſolve to know my imputed crime, or look with complacency on the amiable man who had

had ventured to ſuggeſt the unforeſeen danger.—It was the utmoſt effort of my reaſon to govern this unworthy impulſe.

The eſtimable Murray was ſenſible of an equal conſtraint, and, by the generous confuſion with which he appeared before me, reſtored my mind to its dignity and compoſure. His mourning, and the tears which followed the name of his loſt royal maſter, drew forth mine, and at once blended our feelings. Sir David, with infinite delicacy and addreſs, entered into the Prince of Wales's ſingular illneſs, as well as the various opinions his death had given riſe to:—but how did my ſoul freeze with horror to learn that there were many (and among them ſome of his phyſicians) who believed him poiſoned! The killing grief ſuch a ſuſpicion muſt at a more tranquil moment have cauſed, vaniſhed, however, at once before the confuſed and rapid ſenſations his following diſcourſe occaſioned.—Oh, let me pauſe here a moment to adore the

in-

indulgence of the Almighty, which alone could have enabled my intellects to support so terrible a shock as the report that it was from my hands he received the deadly present!—I looked at Murray awhile in speechless astonishment!—Anger, shame, and horror, divided and tore me in pieces.—I scarce heard his prayers and adjurations, but, pushing him from my feet, shut up every indignant sense in my swelling heart, and only hoped it might burst with the deep convulsion.

A considerable time elapsed ere I was enough recovered to inquire into the origin of so black and malicious a calumny. I then conjured him to inform me who was supposed to be its diabolical author.—To this he answered, that when the equivocal decision of the faculty respecting the cause of the Prince's death first reached the Queen, the vehemence of her grief, as well as that of her temper, made her instantly join with those who pronounced him poisoned.—This doubt was no sooner published than it became general; every domeſtic of the Prince's houſehold became by turns the object of ſuſpicion to his fellows, and ſome of them had been weak enough to aſcertain their ſafety by quitting the kingdom. The rumour was by this means corroborated and ſtrengthened; but, as nothing tranſpired that could authorize a judicial inquiry, the King became ſatiſfied that the melancholy cataſtrophe of his youthful heir had been in the common courſe of nature; when, all at once, by ſome incomprehenſible means, the vague ſuſpicions of the multitude, which were far from extinguiſhed, though wholly unfixed, revived with added force, and centred in me. It was now generally reported that the Prince of Wales, in the laſt viſit he paid me, had taſted ſome dry preſerves (a little refreſhment of which he was extremely fond, though fortunately the diſtraction of my mind at that period had prevented me from offering him any) which moſt likely were poiſoned, as his laſt illneſs rapidly increaſed immediately after. It was well

known

known that I had been the conſtant object of his delirious reveries; and every vague or myſterious expreſſion which had eſcaped him at thoſe intervals, had been remembered, traced, and applied with diabolical ingenuity. The ſingular precaution of his choosing to ſee his own papers burnt had ſerved only to perſuade the prejudiced multitude that the unfortunate Prince was unwilling to ſtigmatize her who had deſtroyed him. By ſuch plauſible and baſe ſuggeſtions the eyes of an inflamed and afflicted nation had been led towards the ſolitary dwelling, where, unconſcious of danger, I remained buried in a grief the moſt charitable imputed only to remorſe. There wanted but little to incite the people to anticipate the ſtroke of juſtice, by tearing me to pieces, when the King confirmed the general ſuſpicion by a renewed and more minute inquiry into the nature of his ſon's viſits to me, their continuance, and deſign: no perſon being able to ſatisfy his curioſity, he dropt harſh and ambiguous expreſſions; and that ſeveral of his favorites had ſince urged

urged the propriety of bringing me to a public trial; a meaſure which had the whole weight of the Queen's intereſt. Alarmed and uncertain how to proceed, Sir David had underſtood at this very juncture my intention of retiring into Holland; and, by ſuppoſing me pre-acquainted with the ſlanders of the public, had unwarily reduced himſelf to the painful neceſſity of repeating them.—He concluded with hinting the prudence of abiding by my former deſign of immediately quitting England, as in inſtances where the prejudices of a nation infected even thoſe individuals intruſted with the execution of its laws, innocence itſelf was ſcarce a protection: biaſſed judges might eaſily miſtake preſumptions for proofs, nor have candour enough to vindicate the honor which had thus been queſtioned.

While Sir David yet ſpoke, a new world diſplayed itſelf before me.—Ah! how unlike the paradiſe pictured by my guiltleſs mind!—Thoſe countenances in which I yesterday ſaw only the living image of their Creator, now glared upon me like ſo many fiends.—A horrible gulph ſeemed to open beneath my feet, into which a thouſand hands ſought at once to precipitate me, and my timid ſoul retreated in vain from the danger.—To live undiſtinguiſhed—to die unknown, were mortifications ſufficiently grievous.—But the bare idea of being arraigned—dragged as a pre-judged criminal before a partial judge, had ſomething in it ſo tremendous, as made every other evil appear eaſe. My blood flowed impetuouſly through my frame, and my bewildered judgment wanted ſtrength to govern the torrent.—A malice ſo bold, profound and diabolical, could have only one author, but where to look for that one I knew not; nor could I recollect a human being I had injured, or a villain I had provoked.—Like a wretch awakened by aſſaſſins in the darkneſs of midnight, I knew not but that the hand raiſed to ward the blow might bleed on the

pre-

presented dagger. In this terrible conjuncture I had only virtue to befriend me: though, alas, virtue herself half withers before the blighting breath of calumny! While Sir David enforced the arguments he had already urged to induce me to quit the kingdom, my soul, by one of those violent exertions great occasions will sometimes produce, recovered all her powers.—Indignation subsided at once into fortitude, and anger into heroism.—"You have hitherto only seen me, Sir David," said I,—"it is now alone I can be known to you;—shuddering with horror at the imputations you have explained, I yet dare not retreat unless I can confute them—no, not even condemnation could induce me to fly, and leave my honor behind me—What! shall I blight the opening virtues of my child, by exposing her with myself to unmerited censure? The pride, the pleasure, of unsullied virtue, was all fortune permitted me to retain of the wealth and honors which once glittered before my youthful eyes—nor did I undervalue the most dear and sacred of all possessions—alas, even that is now ravished from me, and one way alone can it be retrieved.—Desperate as the effort seems, it must be ventured—yes—I will see the King whatever it costs me: surely, the sainted spirit of the royal Henry would appear to vindicate my innocence (heavens! that I should live to know it questioned!) were every other means to prove insufficient.—I will trouble you no farther, respected Murray, unless you will deign to convey a letter to Lord Rochester, requesting a private audience of the King."

An idea so singular transferred the astonishment Murray had at first excited in me to his own mind; that my intellects were touched then seemed to him very probable, but perceiving that I was mistress both of my senses and temper, he presumed not to contend with a spirit injury had nerved: and, struck with the dignity I assumed, began to believe I had

had indeed ſomething important to diſcloſe, though quite at a loſs reſpecting its nature. I wrote to Lord Rocheſter (now newly created Earl of Somerſet) according to the idea I had formed; and Murray, having engaged that the letter ſhould be delivered early in the morning, departed with the ſame caution with which he had entered, leaving me alone. —Alone, did I ſay?—Ah, gracious heaven, never was I leſs ſo!—The ſhades of all I had ever loved ſeemed to gather round me on this intereſting occaſion, and volumes of obſcure ideas ruſhed impetuouſly through my brain.—I had unexpectedly reached the very point of my fate.—That important moment ſo often delayed, ſo eternally dreaded, was at length arrived, and the long treaſured ſecret on the verge of being publiſhed.—For myſelf I had long ceaſed to fear—The fraternal acknowledgment of the King could now add nothing to my happineſs; ſince, alas, that incomparable youth was gone for whoſe ſake alone I desired it: nor could his rejection greatly imbitter a fate which had left me so little to hope.—But, oh, when I remembered that his single breath might blight the tender blossom I had exhausted my very being to rear—precipitate my youthful Mary, ere yet her virtues were known, into an obscure and dishonorable grave, where, where, could I gather strength to cope with this idea?

I employed the remainder of the night in collecting and arranging such plausible reasons as should amuse my daughter's mind till the event was known; thus sparing her all the pangs of suspense.—I gathered together likewise every paper, and proof which could authenticate the rights I was compelled to avow, and, on perusing them once more, found such reason to be assured, not only of safety, but distinction, that a sacred calm succeeded to all the transports of grief and indignation with which I had of late been agitated.

By

By a feigned invitation from a neighbouring lady, who permitted me to render her house my convenience, I sent my daughter abroad for the day; and scarce had done so ere an express arrived, to acquaint me that the Earl of Somerset would wait on me in the afternoon.

What were my proud emotions when the upstart Somerset littered my court with a princely retinue!—Alas, the only Prince who had ever entered it, with a noble consciousness, despised such idle parade. By oppressive offers of service the Earl made me sensible of his importance, and sought, by unbounded adulation, to gain upon my heart, and dive into its intentions: but it was not by such a medium I sought distinction. I politely avoided referring either to the slander, or the purport of the requested audience, and only thanked him for having obtained me the ear of the King; half blushing to have gained it by so contemptible an intercessor. I perceived chagrin, curiosity, and disappointment, strongly expressed in his really fine features, but I could not prevail on myself to confide aught to the man Prince Henry had despised. The Earl took his leave with the same profound deference, and assurances of service, with which he entered; having appointed the next morning for presenting me to the King.

As the privacy of the promised audience enabled me to dispense with form, I made no addition to my servants, nor any other alteration in the weeds I usually wore, than that of forming them to the model of my mother's dress; which ever rendered the likeness I bore her from my very birth striking and obvious. A thousand half-forgotten occurrences pressed upon my agitated soul as I past through each well-known apartment till all were lost in the present, by my reaching the closet of the King. The assiduous Somerset, drest as elegantly as though he had meant to charm me, advanced on my being announced, and politely offered his hand——a sudden chill came over me;——I trembled——lingered——drooped,

drooped,—but resolved to conquer myself or perish, I shook off the scalding tear which hung upon my cheek, and accepted the favorite's introduction.——The superior air with which I affected to enter was not necessary towards confusing the King, who, always awkward and perplexed, seemed more than usually so; and doubtful, whether he should not fly the moment he saw me, or at least call back Somerset who had instantly retired.——Bending my knee in compliance with custom, I instantly rose, and, retaining the hand he had presented to me, fixed my eyes, strongly animated by the occasion, upon his ever-varying countenance. "Your Majesty," said I, "doubtless, expects to find in me a weak suppliant, soliciting protection, or suing for your pity; but on terms like these I had never bent before you—I come to claim a dear and sacred title hitherto unknown, but never annihilated. Does your heart, oh, royal James!" added I, melting into tears, "recognize nothing congenial to it in these features? this voice! the timorous hand which grasps yours for the first time, in fraternal alliance?—Oh, sainted Mary! dear author of my being, look down from heaven, and touch the heart of your son, in favor of the desolate sister who now stands before him." The King started, receded, gave manifest tokens of doubt and displeasure, and sought to draw away the hand I obstinately retained.——I kissed, I bathed it with impassioned tears. "Shake me not off, reject me not unknown," resumed I in the deep tone of stifled anguish.—"It is neither pride, vanity, or ambition, which induces me now to publish a secret so long buried in my bosom. By the ashes of our anointed mother, I conjure you to hear—nay even to believe me.—Born in obscurity—reared in solitude, the early victim of misfortune, long suffering had reconciled my weary soul to every evil but disgrace: against that she still proudly revolts.—— The same blood which flows through your veins, burns in tumults along

mine,

mine, at the very thought of aught unworthy—it urges me to affert my innocence by indubitable proofs—it *will* be acquitted, before men as well as angels; nor does the claim thus avowed reft on my declaration alone, your Majefty will fee in thefe papers the folemn atteftations, the unqueftioned hand-writing of your royal mother; in *thefe* you will find the corroborating teftimonies of many noble and unblemifhed perfons.—Perufe them cautioufly, and oh, beware how you pre-judge me!" Unable to utter another word, I almoft funk at the feet of James, and gave way to the oppreffive, the agonizing fenfations fuch an æra in my life could not fail to awaken. The King ftill regarded me with an irrefolute, uneafy air, coldly advifing me to compofe myfelf by retiring into the anti-chamber, while he perufed the papers on which he had hitherto only glanced his eye; though even that curfory view had deeply tinged his cheek with filent conviction. I was met in the outer room by the Earl of Somerſet, who, perceiving me near fainting, ordered water and ſuch eſſences as are cuſtomary, remaining himſelf by my ſide, as if oſtentatiouſly to convince me that he did not influence in the leaſt the determination of his royal maſter.—The bitterneſs of the conflict was, however, over the moment the ſecret was avowed, and my ſpirits ſoon began to recover their wonted equanimity.

The obliging efforts of Somer to revive me did not paſs unnoticed, though my watchful ear followed the footſteps of the King, who ſtill continued to walk about with an unequal pace, ſtopping at intervals. He opened the cloſet door at length, and Somerſet retiring out of his ſight, made ſigns to me to re-enter it.——The King came forward to meet me with affability, and ſeizing my hand ſlightly ſaluted my cheek.——"Take courage, madam," ſaid he, "for however you may have ſurpriſed us with this ſudden declaration, and wonderful diſ-

covery,

covery, reverence for our deceaſed mother's rights, and juſtice to thoſe you derive from her, oblige us to acknowledge you as her daughter."

And now I was indeed near fainting, I might rather ſay dying.—To be at once acknowledged as the ſiſter of James, as the daughter of Mary! Hardly in my happieſt hours had I dared to flatter myſelf with the promiſe of what was now ſo incredibly realized. My ſuſceptible ſoul indulged the exquiſite tranſport, and one ſhort moment compenſated for ages of anguiſh.—A thouſand impaſſioned, incoherent exclamations, burſt from my lips; and giving way to the genuine impulſe of gratitude and affection, I threw myſelf for the firſt time into the arms of a brother, nor remembered that they were thoſe of a King. Never did the moſt conſummate hypocrite counterfeit a joy ſo pure, ſo perfect; and though I could have brought no other proof of my birth, the ſacred throbs of nature might well have aſcertained it.

The

The King ſat down by me, and, turning over the papers he ſtill held, queſtioned me at intervals reſpecting thoſe that appeared myſterious or deficient. I entreated his patience while I briefly ran through the wonderful events of my life, and thus very naturally led his attention toward the ſole object of my cares, my hopes, my exiſtence.——"I have already heard much of your daughter," ſaid James; "they tell me ſhe is beauty itſelf—why have you thus ſtrangely concealed her?" As I could not declare my real reaſon, which was ſimply want of eſteem for his character, I pleaded various trifling ones, that indeed had never influenced me. "Say no more," ſaid the King, interrupting me, "I eaſily perceive, Madam, you was not ſo reſerved to every one—I plainly diſcern who was your confidant; had I earlier been entruſted with your ſecret, it would have been happier for all, and I ſhould then have been able to account for"—He pauſed ere he came to the dear name of his ſon, and ſighing

ſighing dropt the unfiniſhed ſentence. As to me, entranced alike with his unexpected candour, graciouſneſs, and generoſity, I ſeverely reproached myſelf for relying on report, and not proving the character I ventured to decide upon. I had a long converſation with the King afterwards, every word of which heightened my confidence, eſteem, and affection. I gathered from many expreſſions, that he feared oppoſition on the part of the Queen, and his favorite; and was fearful that this late declaration of his mother's marriage with the Duke of Norfolk would not fully ſatisfy the minds of the people, or eſtabliſh my rank ſufficiently. He pauſed upon the whole, with the air of one who is a party in what he meditates; and I thought the leaſt I could do, was to leave the regulation of the important acknowledgment in his choice.—To be vindicated in his opinion, I truly aſſured him, was the firſt object of my life, and I ſubmitted my general vindication, in the public acknowledgment of my birth, entirely

tirely to his better judgment. That I had been ſo many years a ſolitary being in the midſt of ſociety, as not to have one friend to whoſe inclination I need yield my own. In fine, that time had gradually robbed me of all parties intereſted in the important ſecret I had juſt confided to him, which now reſted ſolely with him, my daughter, and myſelf. He replied that "this inſtance of my prudence, as well as regard, infinitely heightened the partiality he had already conceived for me; nor need I fear his delaying the acknowledgment longer than was abſolutely neceſſary, ſince he could not but look on ſuch relations as ineſtimable acquiſitions: nevertheleſs, as he had many points to conſider, and many perſons to reconcile, he recommended to me to continue the ſame circumſpection I had hitherto ſhewn; but that he could not reſtrain his impatience to behold the fair maid of whom he had heard ſo much, and would come to-morrow evening to a ſeat of Lord Somerſet's, whither he

would

would ſend for myſelf and my daughter, and hoped by that time he ſhould be able to aſcertain the day for publiſhing my birth, with a due regard for his mother's honor; after which he could gratify himſelf by eſtabliſhing me in a ſituation that ſhould make me forget all my misfortunes."—Thoſe misfortunes were already forgotten in the unhoped-for tranſition in my fate.—I took my leave with the moſt profound gratitude, burning with impatience to impart this bleſſed news to my Mary; and, as the King did not offer to return the papers, I thought it better to leave them in his hands, than confirm the doubt my long ſilence could not but give riſe to in his mind, viz. that I wanted confidence in his honor.

I haſtened to Richmond, and communicated this ſurpriſing, this happy event, to my darling girl.—A thouſand times I enfolded her to my delighted heart, and found every tranſport doubled in her participation. She tenderly entered into

 all

all my feelings, and ſweetly ſmiled at the eagerneſs with which I ſought to adorn her for the next day's introduction. Yet, conſidering the King as the ſlave of exterior, it was a material point to heighten her beauty by every adventitious advantage. To preſent her in abſolute black, was to recal the moſt melancholy impreſſions to the mind of James; I therefore reſolved to lighten her mourning with a fanciful elegance. I dreſt her in a veſt of black velvet thrown back at the boſom in the French faſhion, with a ſemicircle of rich lace points, which ſhewed at once her graceful waiſt and cheſt to the greateſt advantage. Her petticoat was of white ſattin, wrought in deep points round the bottom with black velvet, and richly fringed with ſilver. A fuller coat and train of ſilver muſlin, wrought with black, fell over the ſattin one, and was looped up to the waiſt at regular diſtances by ſtrings of pearl, and dragged toward the bottom into points by the weight of

rich

rich black bugle taſſels and roſes of diamonds. Full ſleeves of the ſame ſilver muſlin were braced above the elbow by ſtrings of jet, and roſes of diamonds; and from thence her arms were bare, except for ſimilar bracelets circling each wriſt. The rich profuſion of her auburn hair, which fell in natural curls below her waiſt, required no ornament, but to avoid the affectation of ſhewing it, ſhe wore a hat of white ſattin with a narrow fringe of black bugles, and a waving plume of feathers. This ſplendid dreſs, on which the legacies of both her father and Anana were diſplayed, by ſome peculiar happineſs, eithe in its make or mixture, became my Mary beyond any I had ever ſeen her wear. The fond mother's heart anticipated the impreſſion ſhe would infallibly make on her uncle, and drew from her heightened beauty the happieſt preſages.

Ah, who could have conjectured that this brilliance and parade were only deſtined to forerun one of the moſt diſmal moments of my life!—That an inhuman tyrant had delighted to employ the trembling hand of misfortune in decking a gaudy pageant, for herſelf eternally to mourn over!

At the appointed hour, a cloſe carriage came for us with due attendants, and as the King had deſired me not to bring any of my own, I rigidly obeyed, nor even hinted whither I was going. They drove us a long way, while engroſſed by meditations on the approaching interview, as well as concerning the dear creature by me, I hardly knew how the time paſſed. My daughter at length obſerved that it was farther than ſhe expected.—I looked out, but it was too dark for me to diſtinguiſh any object, and all I could diſcern was an increaſe of attendants. I called out aloud, and one drew near, who to my inquiries reſpectfully replied, that the King had been detained in London, whither they were haſtening by his orders. This information quieted us again, and I ſtrove to recal my fluttered ſpirits into

into their ufual channel, by turning the converfation on our future profpects. Neverthelefs, we went at fo great a rate, that I thought it impoffible we fhould not be near London, when all at once I found we were driving through an unknown village. The furprife this occafioned was doubled by my daughter's throwing herfelf into my arms.—It was not immediately that I could comprehend her, when fhe told me that a light which gleamed from the window of a cottage, had fhewn her a number of armed foldiers. From this alarm we were not yet recovered, when by a fudden rife, and hollow found, we perceived we had paffed over a draw-bridge; immediately after which we ftopped. As we alighted, I caft my eyes round a large and dreary court-yard, where a few ftraggling centinels were planted, but neither lights, fplendor, or attendants, indicated a royal gueft, or a favorite's refidence. The gloomy paffages through which we were ufhered, ſeemed rather to lead to a priſon than a palace.—Arrived at an empty apartment, I gave way at once to the dire, the obvious truth; and arraigning in ſilence my own egregious credulity, felt, ſeverely felt, its every conſequence.

An officer who had preceded us, now offered me a packet, which I received as the ſentence of my fate, but made no effort to open it.—Hope, fear, curioſity, every dear and powerful emotion were annihilated by inſtantaneous conviction, and a ſtupor ſucceeded more dangerous and dreadful than the moſt violent operations of the paſſions.—My daughter, more terrified by this ſtill agony than even the cruel and unexpected event of the evening, threw herſelf at my feet.——"Oh, ſpeak to me, my mother!" exclaimed the dear one; "do not indulge the deſperation your countenance expreſſes! do not conſummate to your poor Mary the horrors of the moment!" I gazed at her with a vacant air, but nature reſumed her rights, and fondly plucking at my heart, the tears I refuſed

fused to my own fate, flowed lavishly for hers.—So young, so fair, so innocent, so noble,—how could I but bewail her? Surely those maternal tears alone preserved my senses at a juncture when every thing conspired to unsettle them. My Mary, by an expressive glance, requested leave to open the packet, and, starting at sight of the paper it contained, put it eagerly into my hand; a glance informed me that it was the defamatory declaration the crafty Burleigh had deceived my sister into signing, while a prisoner in St. Vincent's abbey. The King, in sending this, only added insult to injury, since the testimonials I had delivered to him might have invalidated a thousand such vague and artificial falsehoods; yet had it a fortunate effect, for nothing less could have roused my spirits from the cold and sullen torpor which every passing moment seemed to increase—" Insolent Barbarian!" exclaimed I, " not content to imprison the unhappy offspring of the Queen who had the misfortune of giving thee being, dost thou delight in vilifying and debasing even her ashes!—Oh, paper! dictated and preserved surely for my ruin; by what singular chance hast thou survived the very views thou wert invented to serve.—Treasured, as it appears, only to effect a purpose your execrable contriver could not foresee.—Yet of what consequence is this single attestation towards annihilating claims all those I delivered had not power to establish in the judgment of a cruel, insidious tyrant, who voluntarily shut his heart alike to reason, virtue, and nature?—Devoted to self-interest, vain of a petty talent at deceiving, contemptible in every rank, but infamous in the highest, he meanly watched the generous impulses of my heart, and wrought out of them my ruin.—Yet why do I name *myself*?—Alas, of what importance is it to her who no longer wishes to live where heaven or its arbitrary delegate shall have appointed her to die?—It is for thee, my daughter! for thee alone my soul thus overflows with inexpressible anguish.—Rescued, in yet unconscious childhood, from

from ſlavery, neglect, and obſcurity, fortune at one moment ſeemed willing to reſtore all the rights of your birth, when a weak, credulous mother aſſiſted the cruel wretch who was pre-determined to entomb you, and annihilate every trace, every memorial, of our dear and honored progenitors.——Nameleſs—diſhonored—your blooming youth muſt wither in an unknown priſon—blighted by the tears of a parent who can never pardon herſelf the extravagant error produced by over-fondneſs.—I knew the King to be mean, baſe, ſubtle, yet I madly delivered into his treacherous hands every memorial on which our hopes, nay, even our vindication muſt be grounded."——"Hear me, in turn, my dear, my honored mother," cried my ſweet girl, "bathing my hands with tears of veneration and fondneſs. Alas, the order of nature is inverted, and I am obliged to become the monitor.—Recollect the maxim you have ſo deeply impreſſed upon my mind—that the malice of man would in vain ſtrive to make us wretched, did not our own

own ungovernable paſſions aid his artful machinations. Oh, let us reſpect even error when it has its ſource in virtue.—To have diſtruſted the King were to deſerve to be rejected—leave him then to the contemptible ſatisfaction of having wreſted from the widow and the orphan the laſt treaſure of their lives, and let us examine what he has been compelled to leave us. Have we not yet the power of looking down on his throne, and all its ſpecious advantages, even from that obſcure priſon where his authority confines us?—Have we not the pride of reviewing our own hearts without finding aught in either unworthy of our Creator or ourſelves?—For the vain grandeur of that name of which he has unfairly deprived us, can it be worth regretting while he lives to diſhonor it?—Fortunately no favorite view depended on its attainment, conſequently no hope is blighted by the deprivation. Have I not often heard you ſay, a noble mind can become every thing to itſelf?—Let us riſe ſuperior to our fortune; time

will

will ſoon calm our ſpirits—reaſon will reconcile us to the inconveniencies of our fate, and religion elevate us above them. —Mourn not then for me, my much-loved mother," concluded the dear one, ſweetly ſmiling through her tears, "ſince I ſhall never think that place a priſon which contains you, nor that fate a miſfortune I owe to your fondneſs."

Oh, virtue, how awful doſt thou appear, ſublimed thus by generoſity! When I ſaw this half-blown human bloſſom ſupport the ſtorm without ſhrinking, I bluſhed to have bowed my head before it.—When I heard her with Spartan courage apply to her own ſituation the noble tenets I had ſought, not vainly, to imbue her mind with, could I fail to profit by the principles I had taught?—From the admiration ſhe excited in my ſoul ſprung that pure and elevated heroiſm which calms in one moment every human weakneſs, and turbulent paſſion; diſpoſing us to turn upon that fate it enables us to judge of.

I now recollected that by a fond vanity in decking my daughter in all her valuable diamonds, I had inadvertently provided ample means to buy the fidelity of our keepers; nor were they aware of our treasure, as the severity of the weather had made me wrap her in a long cloak lined with fur. I hastily stripped her costly dress of its richest embellishments, and secreted them. Ah, with what difficulty did I stifle the tears and anguish which struggled at my heart when I remembered the different views with which I adorned her!

Hardly had we executed this prudent resolve, ere the man I have mentioned presented himself once more; he was young—not unpleasing—had an air of integrity and profound respect, that a little prepossessed me in his favor, even under all the disadvantages attending our meeting. Our countenances were now calmed, and our resolutions taken.—He appeared surprised alike with this transition, and the beauty of my daughter, whose

whoſe magnificent but diſordered dreſs had a ſhare of his attention.—He was flattered with our civility, and aſſured us "that every accommodation conſiſtent with the ſtrict orders of the King he ſhould take pleaſure in ſupplying us with; and would, with our permiſſion, make us acquainted with our new home." He then produced ſome keys which opened double doors at the farther end of the large room we were in, and conducted us into a chamber neat and commodious enough.—The keys, he informed us, were committed ſolely to his charge; and that whenever inclination or convenience induced us to change our apartment, we had only to touch a ſpring he pointed out, when he would attend, and unlock the intermediate doors.—The purport of this extreme caution was very obvious; it excluded every poſſibility of winning over a female ſervant, as all the domeſtic offices would now of courſe be performed in either room while we occupied the other; nor was he ſuffered to

ſupply

ſupply us pen, ink, or paper. As the conveniencies of theſe apartments, and the air of reſpect in our guard, ſhewed ſome attention had been paid to our welfare, as well as the moſt judicious precautions taken to prevent our enlargement, I neither imputed the one or the other to the King, but rather both to his cunning favorite. My inquiries were interrupted by the entrance of two ſervants, who ſet out an elegant ſupper, of which neither my daughter or myſelf had ſpirits to partake. Reſolved however to gather all I could from my attendant, ere another ſhould be put in his place, or ſuſpicion make him dumb, I aſked the name of the Caſtle, and its owner; but to theſe queſtions he declared himſelf enjoined to refuſe replying; nevertheleſs, I conjectured from his looks that I did not err in ſuppoſing Somerſet directed him. The refined artifice of offering to introduce me to the King, and even remaining by my ſide, while perhaps my ruin was effecting by his will, ſeemed entirely conſiſtent with the character Prince Henry had given me of that worthleſs favorite; though I could find no crime in my own conduct that could poſſibly irritate him to bury us thus alive, unleſs indeed our attachment to that lamented royal youth appeared a ſufficient one.

In the gallery leading to our apartment, I obſerved a centinel planted, from whom we were ſhut by double doors ſafely locked; perceiving we were thus effectually excluded from every hope, and chance of freedom, I deſired to paſs at once into a chamber, where I did not flatter myſelf I ſhould find reſt.

My firſt employment on riſing was to examine the windows, as well as the view from them; they were ſo cloſely grated as to convince me that however comfortable our reſidence, it was ſtill a priſon. The apartments we occupied formed one ſide of a quadrangle of old buildings, moſt probably barracks, but now entirely deſerted. On making the ſignal,

Dunlop

Dunlop (for ſo was our guard called) readily attended, and we paſſed into the other room where we found breakfaſt ready. Trunks containing all kinds of apparel had been placed there, and Dunlop recommended to us to form our minds to paſſing the remainder of our days in confinement. I did not ſubmit to hear this, without demanding the authority by which he acted. He produced an order, ſigned by the King, ſtrictly enjoining him to keep us in ſafety, and beware we neither wrote or received a letter, or indeed held any kind of communication with the world.—While he ſpoke I examined every lineament of his countenance, but fidelity was written there in ſuch legible characters, that I dared not make any effort to bribe him, leſt if it failed he ſhould publiſh that I had the means, which might in a moment utterly impoveriſh me.

A few weariſome uniform days only had elapſed when every hope decayed, and my ſpirits flagged at once.—Alas,

my

my mind had no longer the vivifying ardor, the inexhaustible resources of unbroken youth——its bloom had passed away like a shadow, and all its fire evaporated.—The woful realities of life had dissipated the bright illusions of imagination.—Every human good was, in my estimation, shrunk into so small a compass, that freedom constituted a very essential part of my little possessions.—I was no longer able to rely upon contingencies, and sunk at once under all the sadness of knowledge.—Not denied the relief of books, I pored over them in vain; every idea was still pursuing an absent good, and my senses would reject the sublimest author, to follow the careless steps of a weary centinel, or listen to his whistling. Whether my daughter had really more resolution than myself, or only assumed the appearance of it to save me from despair, was a point I could not ascertain; but the complacency of her mind and manners was invariable. By a thousand little affectionate artifices she engaged me to work while she read, or read while ſhe worked, nor would perceive thoſe melancholy reveries it was impoſſible to overlook. I was not, however, thankleſs for the bleſſing left me. That my eyes opened on her every morning, ſtill made me bleſs it; and in compoſing myſelf to ſleep, I nightly praiſed the God who yet ſuffered her to reſt by me.

Two tedious months elapſed in undeciſive projects.—Dunlop ever preſent, vigilant, and reſpectful, precluded alike complaint and temptation; but as if to guard himſelf againſt the latter, I took notice that he now never remained one moment alone with us.

The impoſſibility of forming any judgment of our centinels while divided from them by double doors, and the danger of a fruitleſs effort to ſeduce one, had at intervals engroſſed my attention; but the mind cannot dwell for ever on a ſingle idea, or a remote and uncertain project. Wearied out with this, another ſuddenly came to my relief. Though yet early in the ſpring, the weather was uncommonly beautiful, and the lenity with which we were treated left me not without hopes of being allowed, under rigid limitations, the liberty of walking in whatever gardens the castle-walls enclosed. By this means I could examine the countenances of our centinels, and if I saw one in whom humanity was not quite extinct, I thought I might find some means to shew him a jewel; thus proving I could largely recompense him, should he have the courage to assist us. Nor did my lameness wholly deprive me of the power of walking, though it prevented my enjoying the liberty.—After considering this plan in every possible light, I saw nothing to forbid the attempt, and ventured the request.—A few anxious days elapsed ere I had the satisfaction of finding it was granted, on as good terms as I could hope. Dunlop acquainted me, we must walk separately, that the person confined might be a check upon her that was liberated; who should not remain in the garden more than an hour, nor quit his ſight one moment. Theſe reſtrictions were as moderate as I could expect, and I eagerly prepared to profit by the granted permiſſion, ere I ventured my daughter: certain I ſhould at leaſt diſcover the ſtrength, height, and ſituation of the Caſtle.—Dunlop, followed by two other men, attended upon me. I caſt an eager eye on the centinel I paſſed in the gallery, but ſaw no trace of ſenſe, feeling, or curioſity in his. The little garden was in ſo antique a ſtyle, and ruinous a condition, as plainly proved that this diſmantled building was now only a priſon, whatever its former diſtinction. The wall around it appeared decayed, and not very high—it looked down on a moat, apparently dry.—From one part of the terrace I caught the corner of a tower I fancied belonged to Windſor Caſtle, but dared not venture a word which might imply deſign, and returned without aſking a ſingle queſtion. My daughter now took her turn; and, as we continued to claim

this

this relief whenever the weather favored, I fancied it improved her health as well as my own.

It chanced at length, I one day found a centinel on guard whose eye expressed both pity and curiosity.—Mine addressed itself to him in a most pointed manner. Without altering the position of my hand (in which I always carried a diamond for that purpose) I opened it, and the soldier, as I wished, surveyed the jewel.—I turned my head at the instant Dunlop was unlocking the door, and the centinel shook his emphatically. Yet only to have been understood revived at once my spirits, and my hopes; for to escape did not appear so impracticable to me, as to gain an assistant. I saw him no more for a week, but soon found that day was the periodical one for his attendance.—Involved in a thousand plots, the want of pen and ink seemed to condemn them all to inhabit only my brain, when at once I discovered a substitute for those useful articles. From the middle of a large book, which we had unmolested poſſeſſion of, I took ſome of the printed leaves, and from the concluſion a blank one; out of the firſt I cut ſuch words as ſimply conveyed my meaning, and ſewed them on the laſt.—"Aſſiſt us to eſcape, and we will make your fortune," was the ſubſtance of this ſingular but important billet. To aſcertain my ability to realize this promiſe, I wrapt in it a diamond of ſome value, and carried both ever in my hand, ſtill hoping fortune would enable me for one moment to miſlead the attention of my guards; but, alas, Dunlop far from relaxing his vigilance, continually increaſed it. The two men who followed him in the garden now attended to my door; remaining as ſpies on me while Dunlop opened it. Thus circumſtanced, I could not make the ſlighteſt overture without being liable to detection, and I dreaded awakening the moſt diſtant doubt, leſt it ſhould condemn us to a more rigorous confinement.—One favorable omen alone

oc-

occurred.—The ſoldier I had ſelected clearly underſtood me. I ſaw his eye ever anxiouſly fixed on my hand, as if eager to transfer its contents to his own; nor had I ceaſed to flatter myſelf I ſhould yet do ſo, when an unforeſeen incident at once annihilated every hope and project, and plunged me in the deepeſt ſorrow.

I had always counted the moments of my daughter's abſence, and nothing but the conviction that air and exerciſe were neceſſary towards her health, could have enabled me to ſupport it. What then became of me when one day I found her walk unuſually lengthened!—I endeavoured to perſuade myſelf that my fears foreran the danger.—But more than twice the uſual time had certainly elapſed; nor dared I venture an inquiry, leſt I ſhould ſuggeſt a hint to my perſecutors which hitherto had eſcaped them. The hours thus paſſed on, but Mary returned not—Ah me! While my weak hand repeats this, I almoſt expire under the recollection.—Every evil my untoward fate had yet teemed with became peace, nay pleaſure, on a compariſon with this.—Though the turbulence of each ſucceeding ſtorm had ſwept away invaluable treaſures, ſomething yet remained my weary ſoul might cling to.—This ſingle gem, this ſolitary relique of all my fortunes, more dear, more precious from becoming ſo, a dreadful a deceitful calm had at length ſwallowed up even while I was fearleſs of the danger.—Heart-ſtruck—incapable at once either of diſtinguiſhing, or complaining, my reſpiration became perturbed, and deep.—A ſtill agony, more dreadful than the wildeſt tumults of the paſſions, numbed my very ſoul; every hair ſeemed to ſtart from, and pierce my too-ſenſible brain; while drops, cold as thoſe of death, chaſed one another down my ſcarcely throbbing temples.—When Dunlop preſented himſelf, I roſe not from the earth, I uttered not a ſyllable; but lifting an eye to him which would have melted a ſavage, he

turned

turned away, unable to ſupport the ſhock, and offered me ſome order from the King, bewailing at the ſame moment the painful duty impoſed on him. This rouſed my torpid ſpirits—I tore it indignantly into a thouſand atoms; reſentment reſtored my ſpeech.—I called for my Mary in the moſt piercing accents—nothing could ſuſpend, or mitigate my anguiſh. I bitterly reproached Dunlop with tearing the beauteous innocent from her mother's boſom, only to deliver her up to aſſaſſins—In vain he declared himſelf incapable of ſuch villainy, and acting under the orders of the King—In vain he aſſured me that ſhe was only removed to another apartment, ſafe, and unhurt. My ſoul rejected all his aſſertions.—Mary—Mary—Mary!—was all my convulſed lips could utter, or my diſconſolate ſoul dictate.

Ah, God! the ſolitude that ſucceeded! Food, light, air, nay even life itſelf, became nauſeous and inſupportable.—Stretched on the cold ground—drenched in my own tears, I gave way to the

deep

deep miſery, the tremendous void, this barbarous ſeparation could not but plunge me in.—How long was it ſince ſhe had been the very eſſence of my exiſtence! From the ſorrowful moment which gave her into my arms, to that which tore her from them, ſhe, ſhe alone, had occupied my every ſenſe, and enabled me to ſupport every affliction.—Never, though I had led her myſelf, through an admiring nation to the altar, and joined her hand with that of the incomparable Henry, never could even that advantage have compenſated to my yearning heart for the loſs of her ſociety. What then muſt it ſuffer to recollect that a ſavage had wreſted her, for unknown purpoſes, from my arms! Nor could I, amidſt all the horrors this idea teemed with, fix on any diſtinct one.

Oh, that melodious voice! Still it ſeemed to vibrate on my ear, but no longer could I hear it.—That unmatched form gliſtered through every tear, but evaporated with it. The moſt deadly glooms came over me—a thouſand times I raiſed

I raiſed my raſh hand to precipitate—the unfortunate Roſe Cecil alone withheld me.—I often thought I heard her aerial voice, and deſpair ſlowly ſubſided into reſignation.

I now exerted every effort to gain upon Dunlop; but, too faithful to his execrable employers, I never won more from him than that my daughter was ſtill in the Caſtle, not only unhurt, but treated with diſtinction and indulgence.—Yet, how could I credit ſuch improbable aſſurances! or even if they were true, ought not an indulgence ſo partial to alarm more ſtrongly a mother's feelings? To every ſolicitation once more to behold her, I received a poſitive denial; nor was even the liberty of walking now allowed me. I often inquired why I was thus reſtrained, if no injury was meditated to my unfortunate child? To queſtions of this kind he never anſwered, but left me to my own fluctuating conjectures: They were ſo numerous and frightful, that conviction could hardly aggravate the evil. Nevertheleſs, as Dunlop ſeemed

ever

ever anxious to compofe my mind by reiterated affurances of my poor girl's fafety, and as there was an air of candour in all he uttered, I began at length to conclude that the contemptible Somerfet had afpired to the niece of his mafter, but from being already married to the divorced Countefs of Effex, had not dared to avow his paffion. I recollected too late the fingularity of his being with Prince Henry when firft we beheld that amiable youth;—the affiduous refpect he had fhewn in waiting on me at Richmond;—the affected offer of his intereft with a tyrant whofe will he fo well knew how to make fubfervient to his own;—the combination of refined arts by which we had been led to throw ourfelves into the prifon felected for us;—and, finally, that the prifon was probably a houfe of his own.—Through the whole of this, as well as the manner in which we were guarded, there was a policy too minute for a King to plan, and too watchful to be the work of an indifferent perfon.—When by a juft turn of thought we infenfibly

un-

unravel any hitherto inexplicable event, how does the mind disdain its former blindness! I now considered with wonder my long want of perspicacity, and found something every moment to corroborate and strengthen the idea I had adopted.

To fix on any thing certain appears to the exhausted soul a degree of relief; and though, at some moments, I dreaded art and violence might be employed, if gentle methods failed to undermine the virtue of my sweet girl, yet I much oftener flattered myself that she could not inspire a passion so gross and unworthy; and knew her soul superior to every other seduction. From the instant I ventured once more to hope, all my plans for escaping revived; I had no longer, it is true, the privilege of passing beyond my apartment, but misery is ever ingenious, and I was pre-informed of the days when the compassionate centinel guarded the door; nay, I fancied I often heard him draw near, attracted by my sighs and groans.— The note I had formerly prepared was yet in being; I ſewed it to a long thin ſlip of whalebone, and, on the day when he uſed to be attending, worked it gently under both doors, at a time when I judged no other perſon near, and ſoftly rapped at the inner one. A ſweet hope rekindled in my heart as I felt it drawn out of my hand. I watched in vain the whole tedious day for a reply, and often fancied my effort had been betrayed to Dunlop; but as I did not perceive any alteration in his countenance, I became reaſſured; and concluded that the ſoldier could not write, nor perhaps even read, and if ſo, a whole week muſt neceſſarily elapſe ere I could learn his reſolutions. The expiration of that time verified my laſt conjecture. With unſpeakable ſatisfaction I at laſt ſaw a billet introduced into my ſolitude, by the ſame means I had ſucceſsfully ventured. I was a long time decyphering the almoſt unintelligible ſcrawl: "I pity you, lady, from my heart, but I know not how to help you; it is true, you are rich and I am very poor, but then it is impoſſible to get at you; if you can think of any way, I am ready to aſſiſt." Ah, God! how did I lift up my eyes to thee, who hadſt thus ſtrangely opened once more to me a communication with that ſociety from which I had been ſo unfairly wreſted! In moments like this every thing appears poſſible; already I ſeemed to ſee my priſon gates open, my daughter in my arms, and our honeſt aſſiſtant rich at once in our wealth and our bleſſings. Having had the foreſight to prepare another billet, I conveyed it in the ſame manner. "Worthy ſoldier, is my daughter ſafe, and yet in this Caſtle? if ſo, tear away all but the word, yes, and my ſoul ſhall for ever bleſs you." How pure was the joy with which I received the precious monoſyllable!

To prepare another billet, comprehending my plan, was a work of time; with what perturbation did I undertake it! To condenſe my meaning in a few words, and yet leave it obvious to a common capacity, was not an eaſy taſk.—I thus

at

at laſt effected it: "Generous friend, win over him who guards my daughter's door, while you are at mine, and I will ſhare with both of you the rich jewels I poſſeſs, of which you ſaw only the ſmalleſt. Obſerve the form of the keys Dunlop brings —buy many as near them as poſſible, and ſo various that ſome may certainly fit.—Procure likewiſe two regimental ſuits, that we may paſs the centinels unqueſtioned; if you can raiſe the little money neceſſary for this, fear not to ſpend it; I will make your fortune in the moment our doors are opened.—Reſtore me to my daughter—conduct us to the gate, and we will both beſeech the Almighty to bleſs the riches we will joyfully leave in your hands."

Having diſpatched this, I waited the deciding hour with the moſt anxious impatience; and ſcarce dared to raiſe my eyes from the ground, leſt Dunlop ſhould read in them aught that might alarm his ſuſpicions.

How

How to dispose of myself, and daughter, when out of the Castle, was a question I could not decide upon; but I flattered myself that as we should have some hours the start of our persecutors, we might reach London; where it would not be easy to apprehend persons who had been imprisoned without any judicial inquiry or sentence.——A greater fear however than that occurred.——How if these soldiers should not be honest—the reward we must bestow would prove what we possessed, and our lives might be the forfeit. Yet such was my desperate state, that even this reasonable apprehension did not induce me one moment to hesitate.

The appointed time revolved, and I received another billet. "Be ready when all is quiet—every thing is prepared if any of the keys fit. My comrade and self must go with you to secure our own safety, but it will likewise secure yours." Oh, how did my heart bound at this happy intelligence!—my languor, my lameness, all was forgotten. Maternal love, and habitual fear, seemed to wing me with supernatural powers.

As the important moment approached, I knelt and devoutly invoked the assistance of heaven. Ah! not in vain; for the first effort of the soldiers was successful. I reached out a rich and ready hand to each.—They received the contents with extreme satisfaction, and, conjuring me to preserve the most profound silence, locked the doors, and led me to the further side of the Castle. At the threshold of my daughter's apartment they gave into my hand the disguises I had desired, and agreed to wait till we were ready. The tender meltings mothers only know thrilled through my heart, and sweetened every apprehension, as I gently made my way from a dark room towards one where I saw lights still burning: but fearful of alarming my sweet girl, I hesitated at the door. What was my astonishment to perceive that the apartment was gay, magnificent, and illuminated!—I thought at first that anxiety had bewildered my faculties,

but

but their truth became evident when they centered at once on my daughter; who, elegantly habited, had ſunk on a couch aſleep. A writing table covered with due implements ſtood before her, on which lay a letter it appeared to me ſhe had been anſwering. The deadly coldneſs, the nameleſs ſenſations this extraordinary ſcene could not but occaſion, at once ſuſpended even the moſt powerful emotions of nature. A repulſion ſo terrible obliged me to reſt my head againſt the pillar of the door, and ſtruggle ſome time with the ſickneſs and confuſion of my ſoul, ere I could gather ſtrength to penetrate into the fact. She ſtill continued to enjoy a repoſe, it ſeemed to me that I never ſhould know again, and I had now loſt the wiſh of awakening her; of eſcaping—alas, even of exiſting! Slowly at length I tottered toward the table, and catching at the two letters I mentioned, appeared to graſp in them my very fate. The ſignature of the firſt made its contents almoſt needleſs.

"A few days, a very few days more, moſt charming of women, and I ſhall be able to indulge your every wiſh—every thing is now in train—pain me not therefore in thus preſſing an impoſſibility. The heart of your mother is inexorable to me—it has ever been ſo, and I neither dare truſt her with the truth, or you with one ſo prejudiced, till the law ſhall have annulled my deteſted marriage, and the King agree to my union with yourſelf—I live but in that hope; it ſupports me under all theſe long and tedious abſences. Why will you call the ſafe home in which you are encloſed, a priſon?—The whole world appears ſo to him who beholds with pleaſure only that ſpot where you dwell. To-morrow I ſhall ſteal an hour to paſs with you—ſmile for that hour, my beloved, and bleſs with a welcome your devoted Somerſet."

Of what various, what manifold miſeries is the human heart ſuſceptible! None of all the exquiſite variety I had hitherto known, ever ſurpaſſed this new one.

one. My diſdainful ſoul recoiled from even the dear object of its affections—hypocriſy, that eſſence of all vices, had ſtolen into her heart under the name of love, and blighted the virtues yet bloſſoming—fearfully I peruſed her letter, to end every doubt.

" What ages of ſolitude, of ſuffering does " your love, my lord, impoſe on me! In " vain you would fill up that place in my " heart, a parent ſo juſtly revered muſt " ever hold. But you ſtill talk of to mor-" row, and to-morrow—alas, it is a day " that may perhaps never come—you think " me vapouriſh, but you know not how " ſtrangely my illneſs increaſes—it is acute " and violent—Oh that I could lay my " burning head one moment on my mo-" ther's boſom!—Catharine gave me ſome " whey yeſterday; I don't know,—perhaps " I wrong her, but I have not been myſelf " ſince. A thouſand gloomy images have " taken poſſeſſion of my mind! my eager " ear is filled with imaginary knells: I " could fancy myſelf dying. you will "laugh perhaps at this weakneſs, but I "cannot conquer it—if I ſhould indeed "judge right, releaſe my mother I conjure "you, and conceal for ever from her——"

Ah, what? exclaimed I in the moſt errible agony, for at this unfiniſhed ſentence the letter broke off.——Diſdain, ſuſpenſe, anguiſh, contended within me, and ſhook my frame like the laſt ſtruggle of nature.—Of all the horrors that bewildered my mind, one, one alone, could my ſenſes aſcertain.——My hapleſs girl was indeed dying—wan and hollow were thoſe cheeks late ſo florid—the icy fingers of death were impreſſed upon her temples, and the eyes ſhe heavily opened, as her woe-ſtruck mother dropt upon earth, had no longer either life, beauty, or luſtre—Oh, that my ſoul had eſcaped in the groan which followed this horrible conviction!—She faintly ſhrieked, and remained in a kind of ſtupor; tenderneſs, however, ſoon predominated in my mind over every other ſenſation.—I threw my arms round her in ſilence, and the tears which deluged her cheeks, alone declared what paſſed in my ſoul.—Still ſhe uttered not a word, but griped my hands as though the pangs of death were indeed upon her. I in vain conjured, intreated her to ſpeak; it was long ere ſhe had courage to enter into a detail which ſhe had neither breath or voice to go through. "Condemn me not wholly, my mother," at length cried the dear one, "however appearances may incenſe you. I aſk for only life enough to acquit myſelf, and will to my laſt moment thank the God who reſtores me to your arms, though only to bluſh away my being in them. Yet have I no other crime to avow than that reſerve unconquerably interwoven in my nature.—Alas, yeſterday I thought it a virtue.—Heaven will, perhaps, give me ſtrength to go through the ſtory, at leaſt, I ought to make the effort.—Oh, deign to pardon my compelled abruptneſs, and hear me with patience!

"At the moment which firſt preſented Prince Henry to our knowledge, he was accompanied by the Earl of Somerſet.—How my eyes conceived the partiality my reaſon could never eraſe I know not, but they decided at once in his favor.—Whether the Earl perceived the involuntary diſtinction, or was led by an equal one on his own part, is alike unknown to me, but I underſtood the reluctance he felt when obliged to give way to the Prince, whom he left with us—the contempt with which you afterwards mentioned Lord Somerſet ſtrangely ſhocked and alarmed me; yet (may I own it) I ſecretly accuſed the moſt upright heart exiſting of pride and prejudice; and found a thouſand reaſons for ſuddenly diſputing a judgment which had hitherto been the rule of my own.—During the frequent viſits of Prince Henry, when prudence induced you to ſend me abroad; alas, to what a temptation did you unconſciouſly expoſe me! Somerſet availed himſelf of thoſe opportunities, and, by diſtant homage, confirmed the prepoſſeſſion I had already conceived.—What ſhame, what ſorrow, what humiliation, has it coſt me!—Can you ever know a more exquiſite miſery than to beſtow your heart unworthily? to to be humbled without guilt——compelled to blush hourly for errors not your own—and reduced to a perpetual conflict with those powerful and natural emotions which form, under more fortunate circumstances, the felicity of youth! Sensible by the curious attention of others, how injurious that of the Earl might in time become, I requested leave to remain at home; and awed, in spite of myself, by your sentiments, boldly resolved to sacrifice the erroneous inclination of my heart, and received the vows of Prince Henry. To see you happy, to flatter him with the hope of being so, for a time elevated and amused my mind; but solitude soon restored it to its favorite object: Somerset still presented himself, and I took pleasure in the tears in which I drowned his admired image. By some means or other I found letters from him frequently in my chamber.—I dared not inquire how, lest I should awaken your suspicions; alas, perhaps that was one of the fine-spun webs with which love ever

ever veils its errors! I found him regularly informed of all our deſigns;—I knew it was in his power to croſs them by a word; and I began to eſteem him for daring to be ſilent. During the laſt progreſs of the King, Somerſet reſolved to profit by the abſence of Henry, and, apprized of the interviews we granted the Prince in the pavilion in the garden, as well as of my habit of ſitting there, he determined to take the chance of pleading his cauſe. My ſtay was by the riſing of the moon unuſually prolonged on the evening he had ſelected to preſent himſelf before me. The pale light ſerved only to ſhadow out his form—any human one muſt at ſuch a moment have appalled me.—I ſhrieked, and was half-fainting when the ſound of his voice diſſipated my terror. Surpriſe, perhaps joy, that inſtantaneous confidence we ever repoſe in the object beloved, doubtleſs reaſſured him. I was ſcarce conſcious I had granted the audience he demanded, till he fell at my feet to thank me. The manner in which he avowed his passion, made me sensible too late that I had ill-disguised my own; I know not whether I should have had resolution to attempt doing so much longer, had not our conversation been suddenly interrupted by Henry. The Prince to my inexpressible dismay, entered the pavilion.—My voice had drawn him thither, but the sound of Somerset's made him retreat in contemptuous silence. The Earl would have followed, but I caught his arm and obstinately withheld him:—then conjuring him to hasten to his boat, I flew after the Prince. Henry had thrown himself on the seat near the terrace; but, sensible of the necessity of separating him and the Earl at such a crisis, I entreated the Prince to protect me to the house. The light of the moon enabled me to judge from his bewildered air of the distraction of his mind. I had not courage to break a silence he voluntarily maintained: yet to part under appearances so equivocal was impossible. I hesitated at length a faint explanation.

nation. "Could you contradict the evidence of my senses, madam," sighed the Prince, in a low and tender tone, "I might wish to hear you: as it is, spare me, I conjure you, on a subject so hateful, I have nothing to reproach you with but a reserve which led me to deceive myself.—Adieu, I promise you inviolable silence.—He who once hoped to constitute your felicity, disdains to interfere with it. Yet one truth I ought perhaps to apprize you of. your happy, your favored lover is married; think not I wish to reap any advantage from this information—never more shall I breathe a vow at your feet—Oh, Mary! you have undone me!" He wrung my hands in an agony of passion, and rushed through the garden to conceal the sobs which continued to pierce my heart through my ear. What a night did I pass!—sad prelude to so many miserable ones. I readily absented myself the next day at the Prince's usual hour of visiting us. I never saw him afterwards without pain, humiliation,

and

and conſtraint; though he omitted nothing likely to reconcile me to myſelf. During the fatal illneſs into which he fell, how continually did my heart reproach me with increaſing, if not cauſing it! and how deeply was my injuſtice to his merit puniſhed, in the mortifying conviction that Somerſet had dared to deceive me!—What prayers did I offer up for Henry's recovery——What vows to atone for my error, by a life devoted to him! Alas, I was not worthy a lover ſo noble; and heaven recalled his purer eſſence, while yet unſullied. The ſenſe of a hopeleſs and unworthy paſſion mingled with the deep grief I could not but feel for his loſs. A ſickneſs and diſguſt ſucceeded—rank, royalty, diſtinction, every worldly advantage combined, could not have diſſipated the gloom of my mind, or reconciled me for a moment to ſociety. I took no pleaſure in the hopes, you, my dear, my generous mother, cheriſhed for me; but I would not be ungrateful, and therefore concealed my my apathy. Thus impressed, what merit was there in that effort which enabled me to become your comforter under a reverse I scarcely felt?—Oh, that my errors, my misfortunes, had ended here—that I had breathed my last on your revered bosom, while yet unconscious of wounding it! When the vain hope of freedom made you solicit for a limited portion of air and exercise, how could you foresee the fatal consequences of that periodical indulgence! In the first of these solitary walks, Somerset presented himself before me; not the crested, aspiring favorite; but the self-accusing, the pale, the humble lover.—My eyes however resisted the impulse of my heart, and turned haughtily from him; but he hung on my robe, he intreated, he conjured,—he *would* be heard.—I feel I shall not have time to enter into the long explanation of his conduct which won from me an unwilling pardon: suffice it to say, that he knew every the most secret transaction in our house, nor ventured to marry till convinced I was be-

betrothed to Prince Henry. But, oh! the wretch he eſpouſed!——Never may you know the crimes of which ſhe has too probably been guilty! It was to Somerſet's interpoſition we owed the prolongation of thoſe lives, the pride and rage of the King had ſecretly devoted from the moment he read the papers he took a malicious pleaſure in deſtroying.—Still anxious for me, the Earl owned he had perſuaded James to impriſon us in this Caſtle, as well to ſecure our ſafety, as to provide us thoſe comforts and conveniencies our royal relation would have deprived us of.

"I could not be inſenſible to ſervices like theſe; and, finding my wrath began to abate, he awakened my pity, by deſcribing the domeſtic miſeries an unhappy marriage had impoſed on him. The tears with which my wounded ſoul blotted this picture, induced him ſtill farther to explain himſelf. His hopes of a divorce ſeemed rationally grounded, and I could not but enter into his views

on

on that head — I was not however able to perſuade him that you would ever think as I did, and weakly promiſed a ſecrecy I ought to have ſeen the danger of——Yet, the prejudice which induced you to impute even our impriſonment to him, ſeemed ſo fixed, ſo unalterable, that though a thouſand times the integrity of my nature tempted me to unfold to you the only ſecret my boſom ever teemed with, I ſhrunk before a mind ſo diſguſted, nor dared to utter one ſyllable might pain you. The delays of Somerſet, however neceſſary, alarmed and diſtreſſed me—I became cold and melancholy; and, too delicate to confide to him the true cauſes of this alteration, he ſoon aſſigned a falſe one. Peeviſhneſs and altercation now robbed our interviews of all their ſweetneſs.—He often reproached me with having opened my heart to you, who alone could thus ſhut it againſt him.—Diſdain urged me one day to aſſure him I would do ſo, the firſt moment I again beheld you.—He left me in a tranſport of rage. Alas, my heart became

became ſenſible of one every way equal to it, when I found that I was not permitted to return to your priſon: I refuſed to admit him to that allotted for me, and gave vent to every extravagance ſo unforeſeen an injury muſt excite.—His anſwer convinced me that this ſtep had long been meditated. He aſſured me that "he would ſooner die than reſtore me to a mother who had ever hated, deteſted, and deſpiſed him without any reaſon, till his claim took place of hers, and he could call me his wife." The cruel remembrance of what you muſt ſuffer, ſoon reduced me to intreaties, and ſolemn promiſes of continued ſecreſy. "They were now," he replied, "too late;—that he could not ſuppoſe it poſſible I ſhould be able to conceal from you the cauſe of my abſence; and this, juſtly ſtrengthening the unreaſonable diſguſt and hatred you already felt towards him, would make you go any lengths to prevent a union you muſt naturally abhor."——To this he added all he thought likely to ſoothe my embittered ſpirit, and ſolemnly aſſured me your mind was relieved, by a conviction that this ſeparation was only in conſequence of a new order from court.——Although I ſaw in this mode of conduct a chicanery and little art my nature diſdained, I was yet glad to imagine it lightened to you the heavy affliction our ſeparation could not but cauſe. I felt too late the error of mental reſervation, and had ſufficient reaſon to think every evil might branch out from that little root. Having in vain contended with the man no leſs maſter of my life than fate, I at length was wearied into forgiving him. The divorce was now in great forwardneſs, and the manifold iniquities of the fiend in human ſhape he had married ſuch as could not but ſhock and intereſt a heart diſpoſed to love him. A thouſand buſy projects paſſed daily from his brain to mine, and often intervened between myſelf and a mother ſo revered. Every hour that went over my head made it more impoſſible for me to appear before you

you but as his wife, and I became as eager as himſelf for a day which heaven had pre-ordained I ſhould never ſee. One who purſued her point more effectually, has ſeverely puniſhed all my youthful errors—Oh may my premature death be received, by him who made me, as an expiation!—How ſhall I tell you!—and yet I muſt—I have often thought my food tinctured with poiſon—yeſterday—Alas, my mother, where is now your fortitude? —where is that ſublime reſignation I have ſeen you exert?—forget the vain hopes you once formed for me—forget that I am your daughter; oh! think the erring wretch this awful moment recals was born to embitter the days that yet remain to you, and adore, even in thi painful moment, the mercy of the Almighty!—If I have not ſinned beyond forgiveneſs, graciouſly extend yours to me, while yet I am ſenſible of the bleſſing."

As ſhe threw herſelf into my arms, every feature ſeemed ſhrunk, and moulded by the fingers of death—Alas! what became of me at this crifis ! her paroxyfms were fcarce more dreadful than thofe that feized upon my foul—every emotion of love, friendfhip, and kindred, appeared tranquillity, when compared with the wild, uncontrolable anguifh of the robbed, the ruined mother. Perpetually ready to give vent to the tumultuous execrations my heart pronounced againft the artful, infidious traitor, who had alienated her affections, and warped the rectitude of her mind, an intuitive conviction that fuch a tranfport would vainly embitter the little time remaining to her, obliged me to confine to fighs and groans all the miferies of the moment. I drew her fondly to my bofom, and poured over her pale convulfed cheeks a heart-broken mother's folemn abfolution.

One horror only could be added to a fcene like this, nor was it wanting. The centinels, weary of waiting and ftartled by our groans, now abruptly entered the chamber.—Scared at the fight of my daughter expiring in my arms, the fenfe

of

of their own danger ſoon over-ruled every other; they urged, they conjured me to leave my Mary, now apparently lifeleſs; but they urged, they conjured in vain.—On her I was ſoon to reſign to her Creator my whole ſoul was now fixed.—The dear one faintly revived; but, ſtruck with inconceivable horror at ſight of the ſoldiers, ſhe relapſed into convulſions, griping me ſtill cloſer. Ah, God, the cold chill that followed! when I found her hold relax at once—the world vaniſhed from before my eyes—they beheld only the fair form, which ſought a grave on the boſom where it firſt found a being.—Inſpired with the fierceneſs of a ſavage, I graſped her yet cloſer, ſhrieking tremendouſly, and with a ſtrength ſurely ſupernatural. The confuſed and incenſed ſoldiers, having uſed every perſuaſion in vain, made the moſt violent efforts to ſever me from the laſt, the deareſt, the only object of my love. Threats, intreaties, art, and force, however, were alike vain——nothing could win, could tear her fiom me. They preſented at length their bayonets to my boſom, and beheld me with ſurpriſe dare the blow.—Perhaps they had really pierced it, but that ſome women, attendant on my daughter, now ruſhed into the room. Fear for their own ſafety obliged the ſoldiers to forbear urging or enforcing me further. They ſeized the intruders, leſt any of them ſhould eſcape, and, having bound them, ſought ſafety in flight. A terrible calm ſucceeded my intenſe deſperation——the blood which had tumultuouſly burnt along every vein now returned in torrents, to choke up, and drown my heart.——The black fumes mounted thence to my brain.—With a grief-glazed eye, I contemplated the pale and precious cheek from whoſe rich coloring I of late drew life, till ignorant that I either ſuffered, or exiſted.

* * * * * *

Seldom

Seldom enough myſelf to diſtinguiſh the ſhadowy forms that flitted round my bed, and always too indifferent to utter a ſingle queſtion, I opened not the curtain, nor cared who was beyond it.—Vague and ſtifled exclamations alone informed me of the danger of that fatal fire which raged within my veins:—Danger did I ſay?—I ought rather to have called it relief. During the ſhort intervals of my delirium, I voluntarily ſunk in ſilence under the gloom and debility it left. Suddenly I was ſeized with ſuch flutters, and gaſpings, as ſeemed to indicate an immediate termination of every human infliction—My weary ſoul hovered at the gate of its priſon, and I felt as if a ſingle word would releaſe it, but I had neither ability or inclination to pronounce that word; and though I perceived that every curtain was undrawn to give me air, I raiſed not my quivering eyelids to diſtinguiſh the two perſons who anxiouſly held each hand, as watching for the laſt beat of the faint and hurried pulſe.

While thus in the very ſtruggle and fluctuation incident to parting nature, a voice ſuddenly reached my receding ſenſes—a voice ſo mellow, calm, and holy, that life yet lingered on it. I diſtinguiſhed theſe words: "Oh, Almighty God! with whom do live the ſpirits of the juſt made perfect, when they are delivered from their earthly priſons; we humbly commend the ſoul of this thy ſervant, our dear ſiſter, into thy hands, as into thoſe of a faithful Creator, and moſt merciful Saviour!" A faint effort I made to releaſe my hands, with the deſign of raiſing them towards heaven, cauſed the prayer to ceaſe. An emotion I could not reſiſt made me lift my dim eyes to behold, if not abſolutely an angel, the human being that moſt reſembled one. At a table near my bed knelt a Clergyman, whoſe reverend locks time had entirely bleached, but it had taken nothing from his fine eyes, which ſeemed

to

to reflect the divinity he served—care and experience had worn traces in every perfect feature; and the pale purity of virtue, chastened alike by sorrow and resignation, had succeeded to the vivid hues of youth, hope, and health. I uttered a sigh, and faint exclamation.—A sweet, yet sad, pleasure wandered through my exhausted frame, thus to be assured that I had reached the very point of my being. Some women decently arrayed in black having assisted my infirm and venerable comforter to rise, conducted him to the side of my bed, and retired. With a graciousness peculiar to himself, he adjured me, since the mercy of the Almighty had unexpectedly restored my intellects, to profit by the indulgence in preparing my soul to appear before him. An impulse of gratitude induced me to raise my hand to take his, that sympathetically trembled over me; but even this trifling motion made me sensible that I had on many blisters, which wrung my feeble sense even to fainting.

The

The women, as is uſual in deſperate caſes, gave me ſome vivifying cordials, and again retired. The reverend ſtranger once more addreſſed me, praiſing the Almighty for the reſtoration of my intellects—they were indeed reſtored, for oh! the recollection of that diſmal event which had rendered their loſs a bleſſing returned upon my mind, and made me loathe the ſuccours I could owe only to the deteſted hand that had conſummated my woes! "Oh, you," cried I, in a broken voice, "who thus ſeek to comfort the miſerable, inform me firſt to whom I owe the benefit?" He pauſed a moment—his gracious eyes glanced upward, and, having thus conſulted with his Creator, he anſwered me with firmneſs; "that he was called De Vere; the houſehold Chaplain of the Earl of Somerſet."—At that abhorred title I ſhut my eyes as though I could have ſhut out retroſpection, and waved to him to leave me—"Raſh, unfortunate woman," returned he, in a ſolemn and yet tender tone, "religion does

does not permit me to obey you—would you bear into a better world the pride, the paſſions, the prejudices, which have certainly embittered, perhaps ſhortened, your days in this?—Dare you preſent to the pure ſource of good, your great, your glorious Creator, a ſoul yet ſullied with voluntary frailties and human imperfection?—Are you not on the point of ceaſing to ſuffer, wherefore then ſhould you not ceaſe to reſent? Religion enjoins you to forget the faults of others, and contemplate only your own.—Attend to truth, and I will impart it to you—reſolve to be patient, and I will pour balm into the deep wounds of human calamity—control your paſſions, and I will elevate them, even under the ſtruggles of parting nature, by hopes which ſhall ſurely be realized, becauſe they centre in immortality."—The Author of univerſal being ſeemed to ſpeak to me through his Miniſter—the gathering tumult ſtood ſuſpended. "You addreſs not an ingrate," returned I feebly, "I have walked in peace through

through life with my God, and fain would I die ſo: though ſurely to remember the wretch, who precipitates me into eternity by a grief too pungent for endurance, with charity, or compoſure, exceeds my ability. If you have aught to reveal that may allay this irritation, be truly generous in unfolding it—if otherwiſe, preſent ſuch images only to my mind as may drive from it that of a villain, whoſe offences you cannot extenuate; nor double the agonies even you cannot relieve." "It is my only intention, madam," replied he.—"Alas, I would not probe your wounds even to heal them!—If it is neceſſary to ſuffer ere we can feel, believe me, I want not even that power of ſympathizing with you; yet muſt I reconcile my divine and human character, by vindicating the innocent while I ſoothe the unfortunate; though even the wealth of nations could not tempt me for one moment to palliate guilt. Have you courage to hear a letter, given me by my Lord, in hopes of the preſent opportunity? I

controlled

controlled myſelf, and ſigned to him to read.

" In what words, moſt-injured, moſt
" unfortunate of women, ſhall the wretch
" who has unconſciouſly deſtroyed your
" peace and his own, deprecate the wrath
" his very idea muſt occaſion?—Alas,
" overwhelmed with grief, horror, deſpair,
" every killing ſenſation, (guilt alone ex-
" cepted) his puniſhment is as acute as
" even malice could wiſh it.

" To fill up the meaſure of my afflic-
" tions, I am informed that the blow which
" has robbed my ſoul of its deareſt hope,
" ſtruck at your life—that even in the
" wildneſs of delirium your curſes purſue
" me, and you are ready to ſink into the
" grave with unabated hatred.—If return-
" ing recollection ſhould ever enable you to
" read, or hear, theſe genuine dictates of
" a breaking heart, do it, madam, I con-
" jure you, the late juſtice of an acquittal.
" By the ſpotleſs ſpirit of the dear loſt an-
" gel my fatal love deprived you of, hear,
" pity—if poſſible, forgive me.—Can you
" for

" for a moment believe that I would have " touched a life, dear, precious, to me, " even as to yourſelf?

" The abandoned woman, to whom hea-" ven, as a puniſhment for all my ſins, " united me, diſcovered by ſome unknown " means thoſe views I thought impenetra-" ble; and, foreſeeing in their completion " her own diſgrace and ruin, ſhe took a " deadly means to ſave herſelf from both. " —Already but too familiar with poiſon, " and with death, ſhe found, among the " maids attending on my dear loſt love, " one baſe enough to aid her in tranſlating " an angel too early to the ſkies. To ſay, " that I hate, deteſt, and ſhun the execra-" ble monſter, is ſurely needleſs—I even " reſign her to your juſtice, nor do I wiſh " to ſhelter myſelf from it, if you ſtill " think me guilty.

" The laſt words of an expiring ſaint " are not more ardent, more ſincere than " thoſe I now utter.—Oh! ſtrive, then to " live, madam, nor let my agonized ſoul " have the additional misfortune of ſhort-

" ening

"ening your days, and lingering under "your curſe!"——

Alas, of what importance are theſe late convictions? When a ball has gone through the heart, we are incapable of heeding the quarter it comes from.——

I could not however refuſe credence to this letter, and, accuſing myſelf of having hitherto perhaps wanted candour towards the author, I acquitted myſelf to him, by affording him my forgiveneſs.

Nature, ever ſhrinking from diſſolution, is eaſily recalled to a lingering ſufferance; but the exhauſted ſoul no more can recover its powers. The activity which once ſupported mine was gone for ever.——

The venerable divine I have mentioned ſtill watched over me, and by the holieſt conſolations contended with the apathy into which I was ſinking.—But who could heal a heart broken by ſo many ſorrows?—That it *was* broken alone could conſole me. Deſtined to turn my dim eyes around this vaſt globe without

 finding

finding one object on which they could rest, De Vere led them towards heaven; he bade me remember that my treasure was only removed, not taken wholly from me; and that every passing day brought me nearer to recovering it.

For the execrable woman who had, to the ruin of her own soul, murdered the only hope of mine, I ventured not to imagine a punishment.—I dared not trust myself with so dangerous a wish—No, I consigned her to the God she had offended, and he has, even in this world, fearfully avenged me.

The pious De Vere shewed, by preserving and restoring my jewels, the equity of his nature, and I made him such acknowledgments as must flatter his heart, and establish his fortune. As soon as I thought myself equal to the journey, I resolved to retire to France, that I might at least expire in peace, and besought him to accompany me.—Not able without ingratitude immediately to quit his patron, he comforted me with the hopes

hopes of ſoon partaking my voluntary exile.

How unworthy the man who won the innocent heart of my tranſlated angel ever was of it, I had ſoon another convincing proof. Becauſe I reſiſted the impulſes of deſpair—becauſe I liſtened to the dictates of virtue and religion, and deigned to live out the days appointed by the Almighty, his narrow ſoul began to believe mine ſuſceptible of human conſolation; he dared to intrude upon me in the name of the King, late offers of acknowledgment, diſtinction, fortune—Heavens! how could either imagine that I would owe aught to thoſe I muſt alike look down upon?—The very idea had well nigh diſarranged my feeble faculties, and deſtroyed the religious compoſure of my grief. It however convinced me that no oppoſition would be made to my quitting the priſon in which I left, alas, all worth encloſing.—— I launched therefore once more into the immenſe world, unknown—unendeared, and willing to be ſo.

My fever returned on my landing in France with the moſt mortal ſymptoms. —Ah! can I fail here to commemorate the ſecond angel heaven ſent to my aſſiſtance? The arrival of the Ambaſſador in his way toward England, though at firſt an inconvenience, in ſo narrow an aſylum as an inn, eventually prolonged my days. His dear and lovely daughter was informed of my ſtate—ſhe indulged the ſublime impulſe of humanity, which led her towards the bed, where lay a forlorn wretch who appeared ready to draw her laſt breath in ſilent affliction. She ſummoned her noble father's phyſician, whoſe ſkill relieved one it could not ſave.—She even deigned to outſtay the Ambaſſador; and, by a glorious principle known only to ſuperior natures, began to love the wretch ſhe ſuccoured. A virtue ſo exemplary almoſt reconciled me to the world I am ſhortly to quit.—Sweet Adelaide, when in this faint portrait you ſurvey yourſelf, ſigh for thoſe decaying powers which cannot render it more ſtriking.

That my decline has been prolonged till this narrative is concluded I do not regret; and by compliance I have evinced my ſenſe of your friendſhip;—I have now only to die.—Yet, alas, it is with regret I preſent to your youthful eyes ſo melancholy a chart of my voyage through life.—Suffer it not to damp your hopes, but rather let it blunt your ſenſe of misfortune: for have I not ſaid already, that conſummate miſery has a moral uſe, in teaching the repiner at little evils to be juſter to his God and himſelf?——Glorious though inſcrutable are all his ways, and, ſhort as my time now is, he has ſuffered me to ſee his righteous retribution. Condemnation, infamy, and ſolitude, are henceforth the portion of Somerſet and his execrable Counteſs.—A ſimilar crime, long buried in oblivion, has been proved upon them, without my having once diſturbed the ſacred aſhes of my Mary. An act ſo atrocious has broke the tye which bound De Vere to the Earl, and I every day expect him. I ſtruggle to retain my laſt breath till I can give it up in his preſence, aſſured that

that his ſuperior ſoul will prepare my frail one for a long hereafter, and decently diſpoſe of the mortal frame I ſoon muſt leave behind me.

Dear and lovely friend, you are now in England.—Already perhaps your feet have trod lightly over thoſe ſpots where my happineſs withered.—Ah! if ſenſibility ſhould lead you more thoughtfully to retrace them, check every painful emotion, by recollecting that I ſhall then be paſt the power of ſuffering.—Yet when your noble father re-conducts you to the home you was born to embelliſh, grant a little to the weakneſs of mortality, and linger once more on the ſpot where we met: the pious De Vere will there attend your coming.———Accept from his hand the caſket I bequeathe, and ſuffer him to lead you to the nameleſs grave where he ſhall have interred my aſhes: drop on it a few of thoſe holy tears with which virtue conſecrates miſfortune; then raiſe your eyes with thoſe of your venerable conductor, and in a better world look for MATILDA.

FINIS.

Lightning Source UK Ltd.
Milton Keynes UK
UKOW05f0641130917
309107UK00005B/159/P